]

Wh

Mario Mantese

WHAT YOU REALLY ARE

Master M responds
to the deepest spiritual and philosophical
questions of our time

Translated from the German by Mark Doyu Albin
Edited by Jane Lago
*Thank you to Doris Schott-Hüfer for her proofreading
of the English text*

Typesetting by Martin Frischknecht
Cover design by Marion Musenbichler

Original Title: **"Das, was Du wirklich bist…"**
First Edition 2008, Drei Eichen Verlag, Germany

Bibliographical Information of the German National Library
This publication is listed in the German National Bibliography of the
German National Library; detailed bibliographical information
can be accessed under http://dnb.d-nb.de

ISBN 978-3-7322-0193-8

© 2013 by Mario Mantese
www.mariomantese.com
First Edition in English

Printing and Production by
BoD – Books on Demand, Norderstedt
© Cover picture by Günther Ciupka,
taken at the Maha Intensive Gathering in Winterthur,
Switzerland, September 2013

CONTENTS

"Those who are not blinded, those who are without arrogance and confusion, who have overcome the stain of attachment, who always abide calmly in the Self, whose desires have fallen away, who are free from the polarities of joy and suffering, are those who succeed in knowing this eternal home."
-Bhagavad Gita

This is a spiritual book, not a religious book.
It does not offer solutions.
Through a variety of approaches and perspectives, this book sheds light on and clarifies one particular theme. It does not proclaim to express the one or only truth, but rather guides the reader directly to himself/herself.

WHO IS MASTER M?

Mario Mantese – Master M – was once a very successful musician. He played bass guitar for the American funk-and-soul band *Heatwave*. By the end of the 1970s the band had sold more than ten million records.

In 1978, after attending a gala evening in London, he was attacked with a knife, the blade entering the middle of his heart. He was clinically dead for several minutes before being reanimated and undergoing open-heart surgery. When he awoke from a coma after almost five weeks, he was blind, unable to speak, and fully paralyzed.

In his autobiography, In the Heart of the World, he describes how he dealt with these circumstances. He recalls in great detail the deep processes that transpired within his being.

"My consciousness was luminous, powerful, and clear. At the same time I was lying there with a completely paralyzed body, without any way of communicating with the outside world.

"Through my blindness I learned to look inwards, and was therefore able to see in a special manner. Through my inability to speak I came to know the dynamic power of stillness. And as my body was completely paralyzed and I wanted to become healthy again, I learned immeasurable patience, and in this patience I found deep contentment.

"Through this enormous shift cosmic streams of light were unveiled, bringing me deeper and deeper into the infinite universe, and revealing a completely new comprehension of life within the universe. A complete spiritualizing of the senses took place, and I recognized that a human being is in fact a cosmic, multidimensional being."

Through this experience, insight was shed upon Mario Mantese, the insight that a human being continues to live even without the physical body, and that, in reality, life itself is never restricted by the body. He realized that he is timeless and deathless.

This opening of his consciousness initiated a resurrection bathed in sunlight. He was immersed in that which is beyond life and death and beyond 'this world' and 'the beyond'. His personality was engulfed by the Infinite, and nothing personal was to be seen again.

To See and Experience Him

The opportunity to experience Master M is presented when he offers his darshans and seminars. At first glance, his body appears fragile and vulnerable. But the light that radiates from him and his soft, kindhearted smile allow one to quickly forget his seemingly awkward movements.

One could call Master M a "non-personality" or perhaps a "supra-personality": "non-personality" because in his movements as in conversation, in darshans as in seminars, no personal impulses are shown; "supra-personality" because he directly and profoundly speaks to and touches the hearts of the people who encounter him, communicating something beyond anything personal. He embodies the presence of the Divine, which he refers to as "that which you really are."

He had an experience and, as he says, transcended the one who experiences. His deep insight and his extraordinary way of being in the moment prompt others to view him as mystifying and even miraculous. In Master M, many have found what they had spent many years seeking. They say that they have finally come home. Through their own experience they have discovered what they were yearning for, what was lacking, and this they get in intense measure, as he truly embodies universal love and "the Great Silence."

The mystery or secret of Master M begins there, in his "enormous experience" of the other world, when he ultimately became his true Self. During the time he was clinically dead and the following five weeks while in a coma, he passed through a mysterious death experience, similar to ancient Egyptian initiation rituals. He emerged with an awareness that very few have come to know.

It was a profoundly liberating experience, which he offers back to all through his presence, for, as he himself says, his being is "to give." The great mystics throughout the ages have testified to that which Master M embodies. He says, "Those who finally let go of the old ways and transcend them find true fulfillment. But in truth, fulfillment is not something you can find. It is that which you really are! You have never lost it, that's why you are here."

It was twenty-six years ago that Master M began to share his experiences to a small group of twenty people. It is possible to read more about these earlier times in his book *In Touch with a Universal Master*. The unfathomable depths of this unusual master are now sought out each year by thousands of people from all over the world. There are no longer empty seats at the gatherings, and the number of requests he receives to attend darshans continually increases. His repute reflects a radiance that is not of this world.

Manuel Kissener, May 2008

OUTER AND INNER WORLDS
Two Perspectives

The Outer World
In our present day, the sluggish footsteps of evolution seem to be moving faster. Massive ruptures in the fabric of our world have become conspicuous, signaling substantial and unprecedented changes.

The problems revealed through these changes are so multifaceted and complex that it is not easy to find viable practical solutions to them. In fact, it seems impossible. The biosphere, the foundation of our existence, appears to be seriously ill, and the effects of this malady are observable everywhere on earth. It appears that nature and humanity are increasingly threatened, endangered to a point where enormous anxiety has infiltrated the collective consciousness of all living beings.

What can we do to avoid being trapped in this self-destructive whirlwind if humanity can no longer turn back?

This book offers no solutions to these issues. It doesn't tell you what to do or what you should ignore. This is because you, dear reader, actually know exactly how a responsible, accountable life could be lived and how it should be lived, or how it must be lived!

The Inner World

Most people believe that there is an entity with the name God, and that we, the living beings on earth, are another, separate entity. When we look more deeply, we see that in fact there are not two distinct entities or identities. God, the Totality, is the only reality.

When this one true reality seems to manifest itself in diverse forms, it is easy to designate this experience as an illusion. But, swayed by this delusion, humans have ignored the fact that we ourselves are the embodiment of the one divine magnificence. As there is nothing else but God, anywhere and everywhere, it follows that we ourselves can be nothing other than God.

Still, God is not something that comes and goes, or appears and disappears. God is the essence of all that is. Those who awaken realize the formless essence of all that is. From this perspective, the world is perceived as something superimposed by consciousness, as something that does not actually exist.

May this book bring clarity, insight, and love into your life, and may you realize the divine ever-presence of that which you really are!

HUMAN FEARS

There has never been a moment on this earth without time and without change. All things are in a constant state of transformation. Everything is locked into a cycle of formation and dissolution, floating between the harbors of sleep and wakefulness.

At the moment you were born and first glimpsed the light of the world, your life began a process of constant change. Each moment of your life has been unique. No moment has been the same as any other.

Life and death appeared simultaneously, and they will both end. When they end, all plans for the future will also end. But that which you really are has never made an appearance and has never touched this world!

Variable, volatile thought patterns bounded by the logic of gathered knowledge can never comprehend the unborn depths of the Eternal.

Change, movement, accumulation, and dispersion--these are the laws that rule this world, a world that you, in the deepest sense, have never entered. Outside of yourself, there can be no world, because that which you see and experience as the subjective world is what you yourself are.

You see and experience yourself. In the forth-rightness of the moment you are the experience and the one who experiences, the cause and the one causing, the one who comes and goes.

Therein lies the driving force that holds you tightly to restless yearnings and old habits and that generates the feeling of an exclusive power within you.

Where does this force come from, this imposing force that ceaselessly searches for solutions and answers to your many problems, this force that compels you to want to know, to have to understand?

You have learned from this force, and initiate all your efforts in this force, your efforts to change the bad into good, to change lies into truth. But what use are changes and solutions, when they merely provide a temporary respite for the ego?

Without final emancipation from all solutions and all that is subject to change, you remain in confusion, trapped in the valley of death.

Once and for all, take leave of the old self-seeking paths, the dull, mechanical routines of your solution-oriented life, and awaken. If not now, then when?

"Dis-cover" the majestic limitless breadth of your soul. Discover the immense renunciation of your limited being, and stop nourishing yourself from the world of death.

What use are solutions when those solutions are nothing more than egocentric strategies, strategies that bring clarity or relief for only a short time, together with a deceptive sense of continuity?

You search for solutions in effects, but a shadow cannot react on the body that casts it. An effect cannot react on its cause. The explanation or analysis of a psychic phenomenon does not result in finally any resolution of it, because truth itself can never be an object of recognition, of the intellect. Only the temporary, that which is not true, can be an object of recognition.

You look for solutions to a problem that in reality never existed, except in your intellect, which itself exists only as a manifestation in your consciousness. The core of the "I,", the seed from which all misunderstanding, all heartlessness and all grim suffering arise, remains stubbornly in place. It is not eradicated with explanations and solutions. And through this "I"-seed, the pure cosmic light-force, universal love, is suppressed and held captive within dark internal dungeons.

You are convinced that you can achieve everything with your willpower, but you are actually incapable of influencing or controlling the processes of the vast cosmos. Dismaying, disparaging events occur along your life's path, always unforeseen and unpredictable, entering into unfamiliar ill-fated realms of your life. The hope of a secure way of being is continually undermined and diminished.

The one thing you can be sure of is that, on the level of the "I," nothing is assured. See the troubles and worries that wear on you for what they are: murky mind states.

No one can hinder the course of creation. Perpetuation and disintegration are never-ending, because in reality there was never a creator, except in your imagination. God IS! Creator and creation exist merely as concepts in your intellect.

In this ever-changing world, this permanently revolving energy field of revelation, you search endlessly for stability and security. You search for something that doesn't exist, never did exist, and never will exist.

This insight is an enormous jolt for the ego, for it is made deeply aware of its long, grueling journey through the internal night. There is absolutely no security in this world--what a shock!

To heal, you must find out how you came to experience this world, and how you came to experience yourself.

The permanent instability in your life--the disturbances in the landscape of your soul--exhausts you. Even your trusted thinking capacity is incapable of changing anything.

You hunger for life. This energetic force that is the tool of physical existence drives you relentlessly to action. You look externally for solutions from which, on the psychological level, you anticipate stability and security. You search feverishly for survival strategies to escape the dreary circumstances where fear, uncertainty, and death are ever present.

Without an internal there would be no external, and without an external there would be no internal. The internal world is the external world, and the outer world is the inner world. They condition and cultivate each other, inseparably one in the "I." Indeed, they themselves are the "I"-power.

That which you perceive as the world reflects itself, however, in something deeper--namely, consciousness. Without consciousness, which is the essence of all beings, there would be no internal and no external, and no world.

The world is nothing but a perception, which would have no existence without the one perceiving. Knowing this means nothing, but to realize and live from this truth means everything! Allow yourself the awareness that you are formless, pure universal consciousness, swathed in awe-inspiring divine light.

Collective impressions of the world are forceful and persuasive; our common ideas, common misunderstandings, common insecurities and fears are frighteningly powerful. What is happening to us as a whole, as humanity? Where is civilization being driven in this technological age? Are we descending directly downward into the apocalyptical abyss, or scaling our way into higher celestial spheres?

The proprietor of all fears, hopes, doubts, and systems of belief is the "I." It reigns over subjective modes of thinking, the mental constructive forces that incarcerate the soul and hold it prisoner in the realm of death. These subjective forces of thought are exactly that which you are not, because that which you really are has never been caught up in the foolishness of divergences.

Still, those who bring harm to others harm themselves, and those who destroy living beings destroy themselves. This is because each living being is the one inseparable universe, the Totality--that which you really are.

Each cause has an effect, and each effect creates a new cause. Release yourself from illusionary attachments; free yourself from that which generates causes. Die internally before you are dead externally!

When unexpected destabilizing events enter into the flow of everyday life, deep cracks in the contours of our vital organism are opened, and we are helpless, horrified, shocked. Incurable illness, the abrupt death of a loved one, financial disaster, loss of a job, social crisis . . . anything that we cannot direct or control induces deep fear.

Out of great necessity, the "I" is made intensely aware of its foundation and its network of attachments. It is deeply shaken, robbed of its strength. It becomes painfully aware of its transitory nature and must acknowledge its vulnerability. Its will deposed of power, its coarsely woven mental existence is called into question.

Be aware that every single living being on the earth is dependent on all other living beings; they can only exist in this way. And be aware that you, as a single being, are embedded within the entire flow of events in the world.

No being on this earth can live for itself as a

separate organism outside this powerful collective movement. Each lives in coexistence with all living beings, and all living beings are exactly that which you really are! In our consciousness, unity appears as variety. Variety is the adornment of unity.

The cause of all problems identified with the individual person is the intellect. Transcend it, and be aware that you exist far beyond everything that is temporary, and that everything that comes and goes has, in the deepest sense, never touched you.

That which you call your life is actually a mere movement, a sequence in consciousness. The images of a personal subjective life arise from a projection out of this movement, the images of a yesterday and a tomorrow, the images of birth and death.

This movement is your restless journey through time and space, through ignorance, through highs and lows, though joys and worries. This movement is the "I", the subjective force that contemplates the contents of consciousness, contemplates "mine" and "yours."

The act of thinking and the resulting thoughts form the inner life of the intellect, and the intellect is the instrument of the ego. To penetrate the functioning of the intellect and to transcend it means to leave behind a form that was always empty.

These dynamic movements, these energies of thought, constantly create new images and concepts according to previous individual experiences and knowledge. They manage to form an apparent external world from what is apparently an inner world.

The internal produces the external, and the external produces the internal. Internal and external are the same thing; their separation is pure artifice. They exist exclusively as reflections in consciousness. Experiences in the internal and external are like waves coming to an end on the surface of the limitless ocean.

Internal and external experiences belong to the ego and not you!

The world of experiences is compiled in the magnetic field of the brain through the stimulation of the senses. The world of experiences appears to be lived and lived through. But where exactly are the external and the internal?

Your experience of a personal world originates in your brain and is therefore nothing more than a construct of the brain. The physical body also belongs to this inner world of experiences. Through it and by means of the senses, you perceive the myriad objects in constantly expanding space.

Through the act of perception the senses must be employed to decipher height, width, and length, for without these three dimensions the perception of objects would be impossible.

Images arise through the functioning of the brain, as events and scenes are interpreted by the intellect. Through contemplation and categorization of these scenes, the events take on a seemingly enduring significance. But the significance or insignificance of life is nothing more than subjective impressions, nothing but restless contradictory voices. These voices and impressions change again and again, alternating like day and night.

The brain is located in the head, and along with the body and other objects finds itself in a particular space. Conversely, the space, the objects, and the body are located in the brain, since all images and subjective impressions have their origin in the brain.

So, that which you believe in and present as personality is exclusively a projection of your brain. The entire manifestation is like a dream, and all objects are mere appearances in consciousness. It is a cosmic dream, where we are all being dreamed and given life.

An enormous essential intelligence, an immeasurable, omnipotent, protective force that penetrates everything: this is the fundamental essence of everything that is. This divine energy is free from information, imagery, and physicality, this divine power creates nothing, and yet it affects everything.

That which you call "my life" is that which gathers in your brain and assembles itself into a form. Be aware that the assembled and the formed are that which you in reality are not.

You generate and form your own world subjectively, your world in which you experience your own isolated being. The projection, the idea of being an individual who acts and functions autonomously, is nothing but an illusion.

What is generated subjectively is an activity of the brain, a movement in consciousness consisting of thoughts, emotions and memories. Can you think a single thought that you know has never once thought by another human being? How original is your own personal world, which you see and experience as separate from the external world? Yet we each believe that we live in our own world.

You sense space and you experience time in your consciousness, but space and time constitute part of the subjective conceptualized being.

So, how real and true is your subjective world, which indeed is nothing other than an assembled structure of thoughts that constantly fluctuate?

From the subjective viewpoint, it appears that there is not one world but rather billions of worlds. Each person generates his or her own limited world in the brain, where they live, where only they are portrayed.

But the Totality cannot be an object of recognition--only something temporary can be an object of recognition. Creator and creation are actually one, and in the Totality neither is present!

OTHERS AND I

You try to understand other people, to analyze them and their words, their gestures and their appearance. You interpret the things you recognize and the insights you gain, the assemblage of impressions and the effects they have had on you, and you integrate them into your own world. See that others exist only through the subjective perception and interpretation of the "I" for without the "I" there could be no others.

With your neatly trimmed intellect and analytical thinking, you continually assimilate a flood of new opinions and ideas concerning others and the world. Through this process you strengthen your own viewpoints, and you are thoroughly convinced that you exist and act as an individual personality.

You view and experience others and also yourself through this rigid perspective. This mode of understanding others and the world seems a dubious attempt of the "I" to constantly fill the inner hollowness it perceives, and thus revitalize the substance and significance of your life.

The question of meaning appears to be the foundation upon which the consciousness of time depends, for without the projection of meaning, everything seems meaningless! But how real are the others and how real is the world? How real are you and the "I," which in itself is not something with true existence? The "I" exists singularly as a reflection in consciousness, just as a mirage exists in the desert.

In the Totality there is no you, no others, no world. The world that appears and disappears is what you really are not. No, you are not the changing current of relative existence. Awareness of this prompts the dissolution of conceptual images of "I," others, and the world.

Discover how, through the subjective activity of the senses, you produce an array of images in the brain. This compilation is what you perceive, understand, and feel as your own world. Recognize how intensely you become engaged and identified with your perceptions and sensations.

Accompanying these images and identifications are your religious notions, your way of believing or not believing in God.

Did God create the world? If so, why and when? Does God have something to do with the subjective world of your senses, and is HE responsible for the happenings in the world?

Is God only the word God, a word that originated and was transmitted from organized religions and their traditions? Did God tell humans that HE should be called God?

One should be aware that the word God relates in name exclusively to the god of the Christians and the beliefs of the Christian tradition. Other traditions have another name for the transcendent, that which never allows itself to be decorated with words.

The word is never the thing, never that which one attempts to explain or describe. Because you believe words and accept them as truth, they have taken you captive. You identify with what is spoken and what is heard, but the spoken and the heard are only indications of a thing or a situation, and never the thing or situation itself.

As an example, take the word apple and the comprehensive explanation of exactly what an apple is, how it looks, how it tastes . . . everything in full detail. No matter how all-inclusive and even scientific the description may be, it is never the apple itself! How then can you explain yourself, or God?

The "I," the subject, is the ego. Without a subject there would be no object, and without an object the question of the subject would never even arise. The subject can objectify the object, but the object cannot objectify the subject. The perceived object can never become the perceiving object; an effect can never become a cause.

You can explain comprehensively what an apple is, how it looks, how it tastes, and so forth, but you will never be the apple, and the apple will never be you. You can comprehensively describe your own body, how it looks, how it functions, and so on, but the subjective description of your corporeal body and its attributes can never be that which you really are.

You know your body, but does your body know you? The "I" can only be recognized and understood in its functionality, in its subjective activity, in doing. But the feeling of being the doer is deceptive and false, as you are not the doer, but rather the witness. Realize this and recognize what you really are not!

If the world is an effect, what is the cause? Is God the cause of the world? Consciousness is the foundation for the energy of thought and the energy of the senses. Without consciousness there would be nothing. So, is God consciousness?

The Eternal cannot bind itself to cause and effect, to accumulation and loss. Otherwise, the Eternal would be temporary, the Timeless bound in time, the unchanging always changeable. When you awaken, all divergences dissolve, and you realize what you really are: Totality!

Humans all have something in common: Everyone thinks, everyone feels, and everyone acts. Seen this way, your subjective world is part of what all people think, what all people feel, and how all people function. The individual world in which you live and act is constructed out of your experiences and perceptions, but all perceptions, activities, and experiences are based on the concept of "I am."

You perceive that which is conceived through the intellect, and you perceive the produced results through your senses. You experience a conception and the willfully produced result and are aware of it. You then think about the conception and the result and continue in this way to interpret your world anew. But your interpretation of the world is not really the world, just as a comprehensive description of an apple is not the apple itself.

The social form in which and from which you live is constantly created and molded anew by your intellect. Ideals, religious conditioning, and the wish for happiness and prosperity, which includes the guarantee of sensory pleasure, are imprinted on your being.

However, the manner in which these wishes and sensory pleasures are experienced and enjoyed must be determined according to the steadfast guidelines and arrangement of social norms. See how the thinking mind functions, and transcend the functional!

How have you come to place so much trust in the intellect, when it consists of nothing but concepts? It is the cause and the effect of your being in the subjective world and the cause of countless misunderstandings and endless suffering.

The intellect incessantly drives your illusionary life journey through time, pushing it forward, from birth to birth and from death to death.

Your subjective world and everything that you believe exists are a massive compilation of images, concepts, and misunderstandings, which convey to you the feeling that you are something or someone.

Your countless thought-structures are currents of movement in your consciousness; they deceive you, making you believe that the world you perceive really exists. But the world exists singularly as a "pre-conception," as a reflection in the mind, as an erroneous image of something that, in reality, doesn't exist.

Buddhism claims that all is maya, illusion. The intellect hears words, statements that it knows and apparently understands. But the intellect is not aware, while hearing and understanding, that it itself is a part of the illusion.

Maya and illusion are words that allude to the nonreality in which you are seemingly bound. But that which you really are has never entered this nonreality, for you are the Totality.

Words are never the thing they describe. They are indicators that attempt to point out something that is ultimately inexplicable or unreal. But all is not illusion!

Universal consciousness, the essence within which the illusionary world of appearances is reflected, cannot be illusion! It is impossible for the one observing to be the thing observed, impossible for that which sees to be the seen. Therefore it cannot be said that all is illusion, for that which you really are is free from illusion.

Perhaps the world is completely different from what you believe it to be, for that which you really are is behind the words, thoughts, and explanations. Notice when you contemplate the world and speak about it, that you can only do so in relation to something specific outside yourself, an object or a perception that appears to exist separately from you.

The world is a shadow upon the soul, a shadow thrown on the surface of consciousness and then objectified by the soul. Pure universal consciousness, which extends throughout the huge cosmic ocean and gives life to all living beings, expands even in sleep and in breathing. Universal consciousness is free from "I" and free from "you." Realize this divine power and be cognizant of what you really are.

You assume a subjective point of view, out of which you see yourself in relationship to a specific object, and you contemplate this. Using the criteria you have available, you analyze and judge the object. In this way, through what you have understood and recognized, you have integrated further information in your memory-capacity. But, in truth, neither remembering nor forgetting exists. Be conscious of this!

Through the perceived object, the "I" becomes aware of itself, and it is through this process of distinguishing innumerable objects that the conceptual idea of being an individual and a personality is born--the active "I."

The concepts of "I" and "others" appear through consciousness of the senses, which is bound to time and space, and through this dynamic an interaction is set in motion. The subjective mechanism of the will, a tool of the "I," is produced, which solidifies the concepts of inside and outside. But this inter-action is nothing but a mechanism of the "I" and, therefore, what you are not.

Thus, there is this world of experiences, which is fused together through complex chemical process-es in the brain, and there is also a reflex, a reflection that projects this complex inner world out through the senses. The internal world becomes the exter-nal world and thus appears to exist outside of the physical body.

The internal and the external relate to each oth-er, and out of this interaction identification arises. Identification is only another word for the ego.

Can the "I" exist without the world? Can the world exist without the "I"? If there is no objective "I," and subjectivity only exists in interaction, as a reflection in consciousness, then the question sur-faces: How real are you, and how real is the world which you perceive and experience through the senses in time and space?

The "I" itself does not exist in time and space. The "I" appears in time and space. The "I" projects time and space; it constructs the foundation of its own conceptual existence. Therefore it is not pos-sible that the "I" itself can exist in time and space.

The "I" is the foundation of the world in which you think, feel, and act. One could understand it as a multifunctional instrument. When you analyze this multifunctional instrument more closely, you discover that it is actually nothing but the active driving force of the will.

"I am" is this force, and all thoughts originate from it. This decisive force of will is the foundation of the world of experiences in which you live.

That which you process in your brain as information is that which you believe you perceive outside the body, and is constructed and shaped by you through your thoughts and actions. One could say that there seems to be both an interior person, unseen, which thinks and feels, along with an exterior person that is understandable through the visible body.

The interior phenomena become the outer phenomena; that which formulates plans takes on a form. Seen in this way, the subtle periphery of the body becomes the instrument for the mental processes and sensory activities of the interior person. Universal nonphysical energy is bound and condensed through the senses, the intellect, and the visible form of the body. Thus the formless obtains a form and the nameless a name.

Be aware that in the Totality the thing perceiving an object and the object perceived have never existed and never will exist! Because the entire psychosomatic organism is nothing but a provisional manifestation in consciousness, the interior and exterior person are also provisional and nothing more than temporary sensory constructs. Because you identify, you lose yourself in that which you in reality never were.

The tendency to constantly displace yourself from your true essence is set in motion through the functioning of the psychosomatic organism. The active processes inside the brain continually project the conceptual ideas of birth and death, coming and going, and supply a fleeting sense of continuity.

The ideas of becoming, dying away, and continuation have their effects. The soul finds itself on a search for a reality it believes it has lost, a search it tends to mystify and romanticize. But it is searching for a reality it in truth has never left.

You cannot think, recognize, or intellectually comprehend that which you really are. Only that which you are not allows itself to think, recognize, and intellectually comprehend. Why then do you strive so hard to become or achieve that which you always are and always were?

The one who is feeling is never the thing felt, the one experiencing never the thing experienced, and the Eternal never the thing set in time. Birth is but a conspicuous gesture of Eternity, and never Eternity itself.

The mechanisms of the brain would seem to be a joyful wonder, for they build the foundation of physical existence in the world. The subjective impulses that take form are as numerous and diverse as the leaves of a great oak tree. But, absorbed in the variety of life, consciousness of life's unity gets lost. In this unfortunate process a manner of gradual descent transpires, a descent from light into darkness and from clarity into confusion. The ego is doomed to follow a treacherous, erroneous path, a blind procession through time and space.

THE WISDOM OF THE MIRROR

The brain is a receptive system, an electromagnetic field that gathers impulses, processes them, and sends them out again. This dynamic operation can best be demonstrated by using a simple practical example.

The brain receives an impulse, which it perceives and recognizes as thirst. With this sense, the thought arises, "I am thirsty, I have to drink something." But did the "I" that thinks "I am thirsty" really ever have thirst?

A biological necessity creates this impulse in the brain, and the "I," central headquarters, reacts compatibly to this need. The "I," the intellect, interprets this sense of thirst as a lack of fluids and comes to the conclusion, "I must drink something now in order to relieve my thirst."

In this way, due to a sense of thirst and the thought "I must drink," the act of drinking comes about. Fluids are held up to the mouth and are poured into the body, in order to satisfy this pressing urge, to soften this impulse. In this way a circle closes, because, after liquids are consumed, a measure of calm returns to the psychosomatic system for a time.

A further example: when you drink a glass of fresh-squeezed orange juice, a pleasurable and gratifying sense of well-being is created, a sense of satisfaction.

Because this sense of pleasure feels so good, you drink a second glass, and a third, with the hope of heightening and prolonging this feeling of satisfaction and well-being.

Although it is the same juice and the same glass, the feeling of satisfaction fades rapidly with each finished drink. After the fifth, glass you have a sense of feeling poorly, even nauseous.

The healthy juice fills the stomach, but the liquid itself has nothing to do with the feeling of pleasure or the sense of well-being. Clearly, the feeling of satisfaction and well-being does not lie in the glass, or in the juice, or in the act of drinking.

Satisfaction is a condition beyond the glass, beyond the juice, and beyond the interpretation of physical thirst. Satisfaction is a condition that has nothing to do with thinking and the dynamic will.

You believe, perhaps, that you can attain satisfaction through your actions, but this is a grand illusion. What you produce and can achieve through your actions is the satisfying of needs, and thus a temporary calming of the psychosomatic system. But these tranquil scenes have absolutely nothing to do with true satisfaction.

Satisfaction does not come and go, and is not an object to be found. Satisfaction is not something that you have, but rather something that you, in the deepest sense, are. Satisfaction is not something that can be explained with words, as satisfaction is not tied to an object.

When difficult situations arise in your life, you feel dissatisfied. You are able to name and describe the conditions that led to this dissatisfaction, but that which you really are is beyond the subjective field of time and does not permit itself to be named or described or explained. Satisfaction is not the flip side of the condition that you interpret as dissatisfaction.

Be conscious that the world exists only in your thoughts; when you transcend the thinker, you will transcend the object also. When this is realized, you are satisfaction.

To return to our example: Thirst has caused a temporary state of restlessness in your psychosomatic system. Through the act of drinking, you were able to restore the original restful state. But this rest, as we have seen, is not satisfaction.

Through both of these examples it is apparent how a multiplicity of dynamic withdrawal symptoms flames up in your psyche from morning until night, bringing agitation. In this way countless fears, doubts, and emotions are brought to life and dynamically activated.

These forces compel you constantly to take action. Your restlessness wants to rest. The goal-oriented power of the will is the instrument and the foundation of all subjective actions. Your will, which is embedded in the limited form of the body, supports and cares for your personal reality, that which you call your life, your own, the world!

The will, which is effective within its own defined borders, prevents the spirit from completely opening, for as long as the will clings to its own conceptual illusory limitations, the being is and remains excluded from authenticity.

Be aware that you are an enormous divine force that has nothing to do with the psycho-dynamics of the will and its subjective projections, nothing to do with thought, nothing to do with memory, and nothing to do with physical appearance.

As this divine power has nothing to do with the ego and the will, we call it spiritual. It is THAT which your soul embraces and merges with in "the Great Silence."

The body is the instrument that allows consciousness to manifest. But a manifestation is nothing more than an imaginary concept. To truly realize this extinguishes all forms of identification. But you must be conscious that to understand this is not the same as fully realizing it.

The field of movement between calm and agitation is the ego. The ego is the motor for the subjective force of the will, through which this perpetual cycle becomes active. These self-activated mechanical processes mold and fabricate your everyday life. Due to the habits regulated by the "I," you can only vaguely perceive the magnificent depths of your true presence.

Calm and agitation are the inner life and activity of the ego; they are its playground. But silence is free from calm and agitation. Silence is timeless transcendence and true satisfaction. It is your egoless abode, your true home.

Looking at the example above, we can say with certainty that it is not the fruit juice that produces huge problems. Rather it is your countless force-filled mental projections. The multilayered wishes and desires that constantly and compulsively want to be fulfilled, relieved, and satisfied are clearly great causes of agitation in your everyday life.

Can one end this problematical cycle? If you do not know yourself, then you do not know the world. But in order to end, to extinguish, to vaporize these forceful, disruptive energetic convolutions, you must be deeply aware of what you truly are not!

The deeper you penetrate the world inside you, the more you become aware that the world is exactly what you perceive and that what you perceive cannot exist apart from that which perceives.

Transcend the perceived object and the one perceiving, and recognize what you are really are not, because that which you really are, is what you always have been. You don't need to look for it, or reinvent it. The world is merely a sensory perception and not you, for you have ever touched the world.

Your roaming thoughts are like clouds of smoke trailing off into the sky. They have no reality. Discover that which never dies, and be happy!

ALLURING TRAPS

When you think about the complex problems plaguing the world today, you look subjectively for solutions, and thus push the problems you are concerned with back and forth in your mind. In doing so, you forget that one has no problems, that, fundamentally, each person himself or herself is the cause of all problems.

Through the search for solutions to your problems, you hope to lighten your load, so you can experience a trouble-free sense of continuity in your life. You would like to free yourself from uncomfortable obstacles as swiftly as possible and return to functioning smoothly within the treasured strategic forms of your life. Here are the mechanical processes that you call your everyday life. However, the actual problem is the one who wants. The wanting being provides fuel to the ego, and the thing or things wanted are complex and plentiful.

This is why spiritual practices and techniques are of no use. They merely multiply the number of concepts one carries around. The only result of spiritual practice is the sense of accomplishment the ego feels in its own achievement. The ego delights in itself.

Everything attained or ascertained through spiritual practice is undoubtedly untrue, for the practitioner himself is illusory. That which you sense and experience has to do with you, exclusively, for it is you that causes, and what is caused is you as well.

The problems that you think are yours--those that you perceive, experience, and define--are perhaps irrelevant to other people. They have other issues that occupy them. Their problems are different. Clearly then, each person is, within the constraints of their own conditioned "I," his or her own problem!

The "I" arises like a superimposed illustration. The fundamental elements of its composition are unknown. It is a kind of draft or design that appears on the relative plane, and then disappears again.

Problems that surface on the psychodynamic plane can certainly be solved, but as soon as one difficulty seems to be taken care of, a new one takes its place. Each problem is linked and bound at its root to many other problems. Within the mechanical entity there is no such thing as an isolated individual problem, because one's ordered everyday life is compiled on a massive template of collected information that include numerous misunderstandings.

Look within these dynamic information-filled energy structures, which construct and order the entire composition of your acquired knowledge.

Evidently all your experiences are also embedded here as well, because your experiences shape your knowledge. Conceptual knowledge determines the perspective from which you see and experience yourself, your physical form, and other physical forms in the world.

The illusion of having a body, of being a form, has managed to seize hold of you because you have forgotten what you really are!

Through the illusory idea of a body, this reflection in your consciousness, you ceaselessly produce new concepts and are convinced that they are reality. Through your identification with these beloved concepts, your suffering and internal pain are born and given their dynamic energy.

Through identification, you bond yourself with what is identified and become one with your projections. In this way you become a vehicle and slave of your own thoughts and actions. Here you stand on the shaky ground of ignorance, debilitated by your fears and doubts, exiled to the capricious life of the body.

You interpret your pain and suffering as an unpleasant result of something you failed to accomplish or understand in your life, as a disorder and disharmony in your being. Therefore, you look for answers, for solutions, hoping that through pressuring yourself mentally and psychically in this way you will be able to achieve a better understanding. You want to get at the information that has led to your failures, that burdens you and has made its home in your psyche, and remove it as quickly as possible.

The search for solutions is a beacon to the ego, drawing it directly into the strategy, into the grand plan. Such a paradox! The ego, which is the cause of all problems, searches intensely for solutions in order to solve the problems that it itself has created.

The ego has been able to achieve some level of skill and success in solving problems and hopes, with the strategies that it has studied and become skilled at, to avert any more muddled scenarios or distressing situations.

But in all this searching for solutions, the "I" always maintains its place in the center. The ego, this treacherous, self-proclaiming force of energy, knows many strategies. They are often adorned with qualities such as fraud, betrayal, nastiness, and aggression.

Disturbances that occur through uncontrollable circumstances bring instability into the organized system of life and arouse strong reactions. A flood of thoughts and emotions shoots through the brain. The intellect becomes active, and through this a kind of inner barricading takes place. The ego arms itself for battle. It wants to protect and keep hold of its domain unconditionally.

The "I," the egocentric gearbox, tries to make order, to moderate, to create calm. It searches for ways to get around and get out. The "I" actually wants only one thing. In accordance with the nature of its magnetically conditioned constricted nature, it simply wants to continue functioning, living on undisturbed in the realm it knows and controls. However, it is exactly this "I"-centered functionality that produces the road of time, the road that leads away from eternity and into the night of ignorance.

Be aware that you are not the functional being, but the witness. When you realize this, then you will no longer allow yourself to be pulled by name and form into delusion. You will be completely conscious of your universal presence.

That which you really are is always new, always fresh. It doesn't have to remember that it is. That which you really are is free from anything studied, learned, or remembered, free from the burden of any acquired experiences.

To penetrate the initiator of all problems is to awaken. Awakening establishes a merging into that which is beyond the mover and the moving, operating beyond all functionality. Awakening displaces and disarms the perceiver and the perceived, the experience and the one experiencing.

The functionality of the brain world, the way in which you see and experience the world, can be compared to the operation of a camera. When you use a camera you decide what aspect of the world you want to capture; you decide the angle from which you look and how to light what you see; and you control how much light enters the lens as well. Then you take an impression. Our consciousness functions similarly.

Consciousness is the basic tool itself, and the "I" is the motor that holds and adjusts the camera in this or that position. Another aspect of consciousness, the intellect, directs the energy of consciousness so it knows what it should or would like to take a picture of, and which aperture and perspective should be selected.

The senses are analogous to the lens, through which the impressions must pass in order to reach the film. The film on which the impressions are then retained is the capacity of memory. When the intellect acts wisely and carefully in the choice of its objects, it might very well record tender, beautiful, clear, and peaceful images of life.

Just as the purpose of photography cannot lie in outer stimulation of the lens, the meaning of life cannot lie in the stimulation of the senses. When the use of the camera is not monitored with intelligence, and only haphazardly set off by the impressions that fall upon the lens, then the result on film will be a collection of chaotic distorted images.

In this way it is apparent how you live through perceived images and impressions, and how the things you have perceived and come to know have dictated your subjective worldview. These images and impressions are fused together in the brain and become a story on film, a film that you direct, and a film in which you are the main actor.

Worlds of images storing abundant information and associations are retained in the brain. These energy structures are fully loaded, clearly defined, and neatly stored, and can be called upon and revitalized at any time.

Beginning in the womb and continuing through your entire life, you have collected an incredible compilation of diverse impressions and knowledge. They remain stockpiled in your brain. Thus, your memories and accumulated knowledge constitute the sum total of your life.

The known is the experienced, and the one who has had an experience constructs new knowledge based on that experience, which once again will be fused into the total sum of what is remembered. The illusion of continuity and individuality is fed and reinforced in this way.

Currents of thought generate and move worlds. They determine your lifestyle and shape your living arrangements. Recognize how you live from your gathered knowledge. See the ideas you have assimilated, and how you have incorporated them over the course of many years, and recognize how you refer to your knowledge to define yourself. You live from the traces of memory linked to your past, and you define your own future out of them. But ultimately, past and future are singularly projections of activated processes in your consciousness.

It seems as if there is an invisible gear switch in the brain that moves the past into the future, making yesterday into tomorrow. But this threshold, where the past shifts to become the present, does not exist, except as a subjective image, a concept. If you orient yourself from the past or the future, you leave the immediate, the spontaneous, that which you really are.

When you call upon stored knowledge, it always happens Here and Now. This means that your past is reactivated and reflects itself in consciousness, thus imparting the idea of an individual future. If we observe in this way, then "the present" is only another name for the ego, the arena in which the concept of an individual life originates. However you plan your future, your plans take place in the present, the present that reflects your past.

A reverberation arises in consciousness, and the world becomes visible and audible. The sometimes amorous, sometimes ominous symphony of life induces ecstasy or sorrow. But true glory is only found beyond the illusory conductor.

The world itself is something enormous, something tremendous. It is not your subjective way of viewing it, not the world of experiences that are collected and dispersed again inside the brain. Rather, it is the essence of all things, the essence in which all creative possibilities are available.

True presence is the ultimate, the most immediate; it is that which you really are. When you awaken, life develops harmoniously on its own, without will, without an "I."

When the "I" is deposed, God flows in. And when God flows in, everything is clear and light.

Awaken. Rise up and go beyond the internal shores of external life. Then the soul can flow back to its true home, within the transcendent, within the Totality.

Egocentrism is the cause of all heartlessness, all misunderstandings, all falsehoods, and all inner corrosion. The hardened will is the fabricator of this shadow world in which the bright and the dark are reflected, and where immeasurably potent cravings are able to flourish.

Through sensory impulses and their stimulation, thinking becomes active. The mind begins to do its work, extracting information from imprinted knowledge stored there. The intellect assesses how it can apply this knowledge in the best possible way, and searches for the most favorable strategies of action. This is how the brain creates the space in which it lives.

Where is your past and where is your future when your thinking is inactive with nothing to contemplate on? The subject, the "I," cannot exist without an object, and without the "I" there is no "you" and no world that appears and passes away. When there is no world, then there is no egocentrism and no wanting and no having.

The ideas of having possessions, of losing possessions, or of holding on to possessions arise again and again. With consciousness of that which you really are, what you really are not dissolves.

When awareness recognizes itself, we call it realization. When the useless is penetrated and seen as useless, we call it Self-realization.

If you believe that you will find eternity in spiritual exercises, techniques, and meditations, then you are like one who goes to the ocean with a jug in order to scoop out all the water until the ocean is empty. The water that goes into the jug is ridiculously little compared to the water already in the ocean.

Be aware: All actions are conceptual and are guided by conceptual structures. This is why the practitioner and what is practiced are illusory, and not that which you really are. In the same way, neither the jug nor the one scooping water really exists.

You are searching. You want to find something. But what exactly is it that you hope to find? Perhaps yourself? The concept of the search and the desire to find must be penetrated deeply and let go of. That which you really are has never been active in any way within duality. The mechanism of "I"-centered willful activity is illusory.

Eternity can never be found in the outer world. It will never be discerned or detected in a subjective projected world. Eternity can never be analyzed, studied, or understood by the ego, because it is not an object.

That which is realized without thought is never subject to change. That is why it is called eternal.

WHAT DOES GOD DO?

In the Christian tradition one bears witness to God. That which is not to be understood, not to be named, not to be learned has been categorized through a set of characteristics and accredited as being a loving God, a kind God, a merciful God. Thereafter come God's wrath, God's revenge, God's laws, and so on.

Through these narrow, speculative, theoretical, and manipulative ideas born of religious and political purposes, God has been brutally abused. The same process has led to the deaths of millions of people. Humans have tortured, burned, abused, incarcerated, vandalized, and driven away other human beings, all in the name of God.

This shows how the "I" interprets and subordinates the Eternal into the abyss of time, twisting images around for egoistic purposes. This is a mechanism you know very well. To view things and behave in this way is the nature of the ego.

Eternity never allows itself to be understood or explained through hypothesis or declarations of faith. Indeed, the wish for a rational verification will forever be unfulfilled. Your spiritual search and your efforts to find God and eternity are based solely on the concepts of "I am" and "I want."

Is God only a word, an idea? Or is God reality? Whether God is there or not is a question born of the thinking mind. Is the thinking mind at all capable of answering such a question?

What is certain is that eternity is not an object that one can recognize, for only temporary forms can be an object of recognition.

Just as the sun never touches shadows arranged on earth, the Eternal never touches the world.

Transcend the concept of God born of the brain with all his attributes. Let go of your narrow idea of God, so that IT can be!

The thinking mind allows everything to manifest that is agreeable and serves its purpose. It is exclusively concerned with itself. That is its nature.

When the functionality of the thinking mind is seen through deeply, it dissolves along with all ideas and images that inhabit it. When this happens you allow something glorious to occur. You are permeated with real peace, "the Great Silence."

THEN WHAT?

Is there a way for the one seeking God, a way beyond the borders of the "I," a way leading ultimately to eternity? Don't you want to know on a practical level what you have to do or at least what you could do that would enable you to realize the eternal Self?

You want instructions and teachings, but no matter how spiritually guided your actions might be, there will always be a partisan expression of the willful ego. Meditation cannot take place without the one meditating. A practice cannot be completed without the practitioner.

All the exercises and techniques you might become skilled in are nothing more than conceptual strategies that have been handed down. They are composed of clearly defined goals and expectations, for you never come to meditation without a reason or intention. In some form, the ego is always active, and remains active. Through spiritual activity and practice, the spiritual ego is polished to a silky gloss.

In the waking state, meditation and the one meditating appear to exist. But in truth, the waking state, which is linked with time and space, does not exist.

In the Eternal, there has never been a cause for action. In the Eternal, the one who acts has never existed. Eternity is never linked with the external, never with causes and never with actions.

Spiritual disciplines can bear fine fruit. They help people to concentrate, to be observant, and to find their center. But in reality, there is no center. Every discipline works by disciplining the ego, no matter how spiritual the practice is, because the ego itself is the one practicing and the thing practiced, the one learning and the things learned.

Experiences you acquire and navigate through with your senses are not yours, and not you!

The ego cannot and will not fade away through spiritual practices that originate in the ego and are learned by the ego itself. What they produce is a harmonizing of the limited "I"-phenomenon. The ego becomes calmer, more centered, more loving perhaps, but the foundation of all delusion and confusion endures.

As long as you allow the ego to learn and practice spiritual techniques and disciplines, the illusion of a person of action persists. In reality this person does not exist. As long as there is someone searching, you will never find what you are looking for!

Lurking behind philosophical theories and spiritual practices, the "I" tries to hide or to justify its shadows and its shady obsessions. It decorates itself gladly with the robes of knowledge and beautiful words.

Awareness, where no wanting exists, catalyzes a liberation from that which busies itself with acquisition or protection. When the concept of the doer vanishes, then the "I" falls away too. In this way the river flows into the ocean, the ocean of silence.

Silence knows no beginning and no end; it is free from space and time. Silence is the one essential, because silence is free from what is inessential, and free from egocentric clamor. Silence is nothing personal, nothing one has. Rather, it is that which one really is. However, silence that can be perceived is not the true silence.

Our organized and structured life, which of itself is bound and limited, does not know true silence. Be conscious that everything you 'know' is what sets you apart from what you really are.

The personality, the "I," is like a shadow cast by the sun. It has no real individual existence. Shadows can be longer or shorter, and move about over the earth, but at some time they fade away and are gone.

Although the sun is the cause of the phenomenon of a shadow, it is never affected by a shadow. It remains, as always, without shadows. In just this way, silence and the personality interact. And so it is with God and the world. You are unborn, timeless silence, the eternal Self. So be what you really are.

Knowledge and memory are born of time and, thus, not what you are. That which you really are is free from the past and free from the future, the Great Secret.

When you awaken, your awareness will pervade the entire conceptual world. This insight brings about dissolution of all misunderstandings. Birth, the body, and death are discerned clearly and seen as concepts, superimpositions of consciousness.

The manifest and the un-manifest are one. It is only the thinking mind that separates them! To realize this is to awaken. But in truth, there is no awakening. There is only Self-realization.

WHERE ARE YOU GOING AND WHY?

What is the search for solutions, and what is liberation? The sensitive one inside you has an idea, a sense of the boundlessness of true being. But the old doubter perseveres in its stubborn rational perspective. It is convinced that the material overlay that it perceives is real. However, the world we attempt to nail down with subjective ideas does not allow itself to be figured out and solved in this way, and cannot be mastered through artificially formulated virtues.

The "I" that causes all our problems continues to search for solutions that provide change and improvement. To implement these corrections, a specialist is called upon, the intellect, the great strategist. Life strategies and other mechanisms learned in the past are systematically brought forth from memory. The information is then analyzed, contemplated, reactivated, and applied according to a particular situation.

In order to find solutions, the "I," limited in its conditioned thinking state, always searches and follows the same paths, since that which has been learned and has become familiar conveys a feeling of safety when one feels insecure. But the intellect, which is the instrument of the ego, cannot overcome and liberate itself, just as you cannot put yourself up on your own shoulders.

The intellect engages an enormous bundle of concepts, which includes countless spiritual practices and rituals. These are all founded by the intellect, then set in motion and accomplished by the intellect. But as long as the intellect is active, there is duality. Only when the intellect is transcended can eternal truth shine forth.

Those who awaken are no longer searching for solutions. Rather, they see through the ego, the instigating principle of all problems. In this way the solution-seeker is dissolved. Penetrating the dynamics of the "I," consciousness is freed from the burden of conceptual misunderstandings and delusions. Thus you realize what you really never were!

Direct perception of how the ego functions and the sphere of its influence produces liberation from solutions. Solutions, on the psychodynamic level, are nothing more than survival strategies, and they serve life only in that one lives on. The programmed subjective processes of life originating in the ego produce and retain that which you see and experience as the world, that with which you identify yourself.

Liberation is the irreversible freeing of the entire limited being, bringing an immersion in boundless deathless being-ness. Liberation occurs in the condition of non-aspiring and non-causing, and not through effort.

Eternal presence is impossible to explain in the human language, for Totality is completely unimaginable and incomprehensible for the instrument of the intellect. That which you seek within, what you hope to find, will never be found, for the one seeking is hollow and unreal.

Nothing can exist apart from you, as everything that exists is you--the universal, life-bestowing essence!

THE DYNAMIC WORLD
OF THE BRAIN

Thoughts of one's own death are born in the conditioned mind, and this one single subject casts a thousand shadows. These shadow-energies, which take the form of dynamic fears, anxiety, and insecurity, expand in the world of the brain. They come to rule and control the emotional condition of human affairs, your everyday life.

The inescapable knowledge that all living beings in the world must die seems to have tattooed an insurmountable black wall in your thinking mind. This devastating fact has adorned your life with tears and suffering. Death, the bitter chalice of time, mixes drab, downbeat colors into the brightly hued canvas that is our life.

The knowledge that you must leave all the people and every single thing that you love sits like a constant, oppressive shadow on the soul. The idea that you must ultimately leave your trusted body, which will become stiff and cold and be buried deep in the earth, or burned to ashes, sends the mind into a state of shock.

These are thoughts about something you would

rather not contemplate. Therefore be deeply aware that the body is nothing more than a thought.

You try to suppress the thoughts you have of your own death. You try to push them as far away as possible, banishing them to the future, all the while recording the information that other bodies have indeed departed. You act as though physical death has nothing to do with you. This behavior is an exceptionally successful survival strategy of the ego, for it wants everything, except to die.

At some point in the course of your life the subject of your own final departure from the world will arise. The intellect will find no well-based explanations or solutions for this fickle topic. A gaping black hole arises in the mind. This immeasurable, inconceivable space, a space all human thoughts eventually collide with, overwhelms our limited human comprehension.

Thoughts of the last moments in the body, of the last breath of the flesh, at the end of your life on earth, produce a kind of discomfort, and at the same time generate a strange fascination. Death appears to be a powerful embrace of cold steel, from which the soul wants to free itself. So, die now, before you are dead!

Is there a life after death? If so, how will it be? Will you be born again at some future time? If so, how, where, when, and why?

The "I" searches feverishly for a handhold in the unseen world. It wants testimonies of life after physical death. Thought-energies search and test all sorts of possibilities and accounts. This intense searching mind-set wants suggestions and guidance so that it might attain an existence outside the physical body, beyond the grave.

The motivation of seeking is to keep living, which is bound to the hope of entering an unknown spiritual world after death, where one can continue on. This appears to be the ultimate goal of the seeking "I"!

But all this searching and hoping is and remains purely superficial. Your searching is only active while you identify yourself with the form of your transitory body and the form of all other temporary bodies. You are not aware that your body, just as every other body, exists merely as an image of the "I" in your consciousness.

Since you are already Totality now, and were never anything else, where do you want to go?

WITHOUT BIRTH

When did your search begin? When did your life begin? Did it start with your birth? Were you there at your birth? After you were born, did you look around and think to yourself, "Now I've been born. This is my mother. There in the corner is my father. The other guy is the doctor." Were you conscious that you were being born? Was it a wish of yours, or was it something you resolved to do?

You have no memory of these moments of your birth, none at all, and also no memory of the weeks afterward. No factual information exists in your brain concerning this time in your life. There is nothing you can truly recall.

Since you have absolutely no memory of your own birth, you have no objective psychological proof that you were born. Yet you claim you were born. You testify to something that you yourself cannot possibly know, as you have not the slightest memory of your day of birth. "I was born" is a statement based solely on your identification with your body.

Apparently the birth was an experience without an experience-er. Someone explained to you at a later time that you were born, but were you really born, or was it only your body, the genetic material from your parents?

You authenticate the world you perceive and also your body, without being aware that the entire perceived world-theater is internally hollow and possesses no objective reality. The subject and the object both exist only as images in consciousness.

The intellect covers the inseparable Totality, and this results in you not being able to realize what you really are, and not being aware of your true presence in the eternal Now!

Only many months after your birth were you told that you were born. Years later you were also told that you will die. You have no neutral memory of your birth. You came into the world without knowing that you arrived. So, what is this "I" that says, "I was born, and I will die" How real is this "I," and how real is the body?

Totality is indivisible, therefore Totality can never be the hazy world of the "I," which in reality does not exist. The idea that you were born is based on the image of two independent bodies, which you designate as your parents. But you and they exist only conceptually – as reflections in consciousness.

Be aware that that which you really are is formless, timeless, and beyond all descriptions, eternally unborn. You have never come anywhere and have never gone anywhere: the corporeal is that which you really are not.

You analyze you own mental constructs, extractions from that which you believe yourself to be, and you identify with that which you analyze.

The amalgamation-process in your brain creates a world of experiences that occur through the stimulation and functionality of the senses. Through mental activity, the ostensible internal world becomes externalized, and the ostensible outer world becomes internalized. The internal and external condition each other. But you, in reality, are indivisible, and the indivisible has neither an inside nor an outside.

You exist because the Totality exists, and the Totality exists because you exist. "I and the Father are one." This is how Master Jesus explained it two thousand years ago.

That which is internal and that which is external, that which comes and goes, is nothing other than diversion in a theater of ignorance. All knowledge ends in what is unknowable, and all vain efforts of the "I" end in confusion.

You search in the limited world of the brain for the meaning of life and therefore call many things into question. But the "I" is the one thing you do not bring into question. This is because the world of limitations is familiar to you, and the unlimited is not. In your mental world you have reached heaven, the highest highs, and you have fallen to the darkest depths. But through all this, you have never questioned the relativity of the "I" having the experiences.

As long as you are trapped in your ideas and images, you cannot disengage and see through the meaninglessness of the search for meaning.

In the passage of your life you have had countless good, bad, happy, and horrifying experiences. Due to their intensity, these experiences have continually introduced new influences and aspects into your life and affected how you perceive and understand it. The actual problem here is that you were never aware that the condition of wakefulness in which you experience everything is untrue and unreal. Your true magnificence, your true home, is there, where you, in your subjectivity, have ceased to exist.

When the limited is extinguished, the unlimited is here. Where "I" departs is where God shines. As long as the intellect is active, chaos, confusion, and duality reign. If it is transcended, eternal truth alights.

With the many life experiences you have endured and struggled through, and through identification with these experiences, an enormous multitude of misunderstandings, dilemmas, and conceptual attachments have arisen. But without the concepts of "mine" and "yours," of "I" and "others," these subjective occurrences and projections would never be possible.

Be aware that that which you really are has never experienced or endured something, and has never taken action. Awaken and discover that the special and exclusive residence where you lead a protected private life has never truly existed, that you have never appeared in this world, and that the world has never touched you. You are "I"-less, formless, deathless, radiant, infinite splendor.

The body is projected from the thinking intellect, and the intellect has its origin in consciousness. The thinker is the cause of thoughts; it is the cause of the effects that then appear. The body, the thinker, space, and time exist in consciousness, but they possess no true reality; they are only reflections raised in consciousness.

See through your antiquated, rigid, and bogus identifications; let them fade away in the sunlight. If not now, then when?

The possibility of having stability and security in your thought-produced lifestyle is an illusion. You know this! The psychosomatic organism is like a shadow cast by the sun; it has no true reality. It is just the same with stability and security.

You have forgotten who you really are and believe yourself to be the body and the intellect. This is the fundamental cause of your confusion and suffering.

The total sum of your life experiences is a gigantic network of information and energies stored and imprinted in your memory. Your environment emerges out of this massive reservoir of dynamic knowledge, where you live, where you are the only actor.

In this narrow interior borderland you devise plans and strategies for your future, but behind the facade of your constructed world, a restless spirit is hidden--you!

You perceive the world through your senses and you identify yourself with what you see. But the seen as well as the seer are exactly that which you are not.

Your subjective field of influence, which you constantly interpret as new, correlates to the activity of the intellect at work. But because the intellect itself has no real independent existence, the subjective field of activity it produces also has no real existence.

The good and the bad belong to the thinking mind and not to you, so don't busy yourself with good and bad, with the seer and the seen. Simply be what you really are! That which you really are is uncomplicated. So don't complicate your being unnecessarily.

The knowledge imprinted in your brain is continually augmented, corrected, and improved, and this allows the opening of the mental field to new happenings, to the process of gathering new pursuits and experiences. The experiences you have broaden and extend your subjective knowledge. In the course of your life, your memory is inhabited and engraved with an enormous collection of misunderstandings and illusory images.

Your thoughts and perceptions change constantly. But you remain the same. Therefore, birth and death affect only the body, and not you.

You are completely bound to the happenings of your everyday life, and commit yourself to fulfilling the various tasks and obligations that are required within the social structure around you. This mode of activity functions with mechanisms and patterns you have learned and come to cherish.

This process serves one major purpose: to provide a sense of continuity. You are afraid of the unforeseen, and you do everything you can to avoid any interruption to your sense of continuity and to protect your fragile feeling of stability and security from being disturbed.

The pressure of responsibility tied to your daily activities has far-ranging effects. Fear arises, fear that what one owns (including the body) will be lost, fear of betraying others, fear of not doing enough, fear of not being loved, fear of showing weakness, fear of an uncertain future, fear of life, fear of death, fear of fear.

Although you know from your own experience that everything in your life changes constantly, you still make unceasing efforts to bring stability to the unstable, to make what is always changing unchangeable.

These constant acts of will, which always arise out of desperation, are never successful. But one proceeds onward, as if trying to hold water with one's bare hands.

When you awaken, all toils and strivings and all

misunderstandings come to an end. In awakening, the one causing the conflicts and fears dissolves into nothing. He or she was never anything other than nothing.

The being you believe yourself to be exists only as a superimposed image in your mind. Everything you experience is neither enduring nor real, and can only be sensed as real by you through delusion.

FINALLY DEAD

You define your life by forming interpretations of your constantly changing existence and then identifying yourself with those interpretations. Within the dynamic field of subjective thought patterns, persuasive illusory ideas – of having and losing, of mine and yours, of life and death – are vibrating.

You forget therein that these inert mechanical everyday processes, in fact all thoughts and all actions in your life, are based solely on the concept of "I am." When you see through these trivial mental formulas, the king falls swiftly from his throne. In other words, death itself dies.

Never was there an experience. Never was there one who experiences. Never was there someone who knew something. Never was there something to be known. What truly is is what you are: unborn and unformed, power without force, the light that sets everything alight.

Where does death begin, and where does life end? Death is the same as life, for nothing can exist apart from you. Life and death are two sides of the same coin. Depending on your perspective, you see the different images, and these are what you interpret and try to understand.

The mind attempts to examine, to scrutinize all that comes and goes. This research is the effort of the ego. But neither the examiner nor that which is examined will endure. Still, because of your delusive attitude, you believe unquestionably in the results of your scrutiny.

The ego is the king of shadows. He has managed successfully to construct a world stage for himself and set himself up as the lead actor. But his play and his theater are nothing but a comedy of ignorance, for in reality there is no actor and no play.

"I live" and "I will die" are fabricated conceptual images of the "I," and this "I" exists solely as an apparition in your consciousness. Life and death are concepts, which are reinserted again and again. You give them life, because you are absolutely convinced that you are the body.

You believe that you live now and will be dead at some later time. You speak of life and death as if they actually exist. You breathe incredible energy into these ideas and identify yourself with these projections. In this way you successfully produce something apparently real, made out of something illusory.

The entirety of the world, everything tied to your senses, exists only in your consciousness, and consciousness is nothing other than the thought "I am." The mind is hypnotized by the impressive pictures and processes taking place in the world, but that which you perceive with your senses is nothing but the dream of the dreamer. Awaken and stop constraining yourself within processes and images. Be yourself!!

The "I" is bound within the immense collective illusion, within commanding dynamic forces. In this ocean of thoughts and emotions all processes take place: origination, unfolding, flourishing, withering, and expiration.

Caught up in these massive and fully animated energies, you are unable to see through and recognize the illusions, to see that coming and going, life and death only exist as movements within the brain, which you produce and perceive in time and space.

Pure perception never touches the world, for that which produces consciousness is prior to it. What were you before the thought "I am" appeared?

The Eternal is reflected and takes a form in our awareness, although within the Eternal nothing produced has ever existed. In the cool light of the full moon one sees the reflection of a landscape upon a clear still mountain lake. But the moon itself has no light. The sun is shining upon it.

Neither the sun, nor the moon, nor the lake, nor the reflected landscape is real, for the waking state in which these things can be perceived does not exist. Nothing truly exists here. Yet there is so much chaos in the world.

Death has no objective reality, because the "I"

that is able to experience it doesn't even exist. The illusory "I" projects the illusory sense of a life with continuity, an illusion in which the concept of death is deeply embedded.

The physical embodiment that acts as the foundation for your many interchanging mental constructions has no actual reality, as it is based on nothing more than the conceptual image of "I am."

You fear death, you fear your own life, you fear your own projection, you fear fear itself. See through these illusory speculations you take for granted, and die, die before you are dead!

Release yourself now from the vague illusion that you are a form, that you have a shape, and realize that which you really are. You were never incomplete, because you have never touched the world. So then, be as you are--free from delusion and identification.

The world that appears in the mind is a theater of the senses, a theater that is produced inside the brain. Everything you have experienced and learned within this theater is recorded and filed in your memory as potential capacities and abilities. Thought extracts information from these memories, and this is where the thinker and the objects of thought appear in our awareness.

This process is a dynamic movement within the brain, a movement that sets the illusory and deceptive oceans of thought in motion and gives them continuous life. Through subtle movements of thought sublimated by the will, your subjective life is created anew. This happens again and again, and through this, the illusory sense of a life that continues on and on is produced.

The dynamic force of will can direct its power only within a limited radius, within the known, within that which can be perceived subjectively. The powers of the will are effectual only in the ego-world. Through their activity, restrictive shadows are made stronger.

These egocentric energies, well directed and neatly tied together, are the ones causing all confusion, all obsessions, and all fears. They tie the soul to the shadows of death. In this way the deluded soul plummets into the deep abyss within the shores of death and believes that life and death truly exist.

When the actor is seen and penetrated, then the reign of the "want-er" is over. Here, enduring peace reveals itself. That which has taken a form returns to the formless and vanishes in the ocean of undying splendor and divine illumination.

Your progressions of thought and processes of perception, your entire life's journey, are reflected in your consciousness, as nothing can exist or occur apart from or outside your consciousness. But because your consciousness is "I am," that which you really are remains underneath, though "underneath" should not be understood in a three-dimensional sense.

Be aware that you are not the superimposed,

illusory "I"-appearance that reflects itself in consciousness. Reflections necessitate an individual who perceives them, one who objectifies the reflections as reflections, and a consciousness that is aware of them.

The intellect contemplates the objects it perceives, which in reality don't even exist. The truth is that your body and the world exist only in your thoughts.

YOUR PAST HAS NO FUTURE

Your past does not think about you. You think about your past. Your future does not think about you. You think about your future. Your body does not think about you. You think about your body.

Thinking occurs only in the present. The present is the face of the past. Within the movement of thought, the dream-concepts of a yesterday and a tomorrow are born; the dream-concepts of life and death are initiated here as well. The present is the fictional location for constructing illusions of a subjective life.

If you examine the present, you will find nothing. It is hollow. You can only observe that which you really are not. That which you really are is not observable. Therefore, be conscious that the observer as well as that which is observed is hollow.

As a thinking, planning individual with the will to act, you cultivate your goals within the limited ego-world. But without consciousness there would be not be a thinking, planning individual and, thus, no will to act, no goals to cultivate, no past, and no future.

Because the thinking, planning individual exists

solely as a reflection in consciousness, it possesses no personal independent reality. The plans and the goals of the thinking individual are like dreams of a dreamer.

Thinking, planning, and knowing are activities of the mind, and these activities leave behind memories, traces of the past, identifications. But in truth, you can only remember what you truly are not, because what you really are has never left a trace of memory.

In reality you are deathless, formless, and unborn. Therefore, you cannot be an object, nor can you be an independent being. Only what is transient can be an object or a form. That which is realized without being understood is never subject to change, and that which never changes is that which you really are.

Ignorance compels the soul into taking a form. It manages to coax it away from the immortal and toward the mortal, away from light and into the shadows. Because you identify yourself with the body, you are utterly convinced that, at some unknown time in an unknown future, death awaits you.

What then will death destroy? It will kill your body, your idea of the present, which exists solely from gathered concepts, memories, and images. But will death destroy everything? Will your soul, about which you know nothing definitive, live on? Will death be an experience you can consciously go through, or is it an experience without an experience-er, where the knower and the known are absent? Be aware that that which you really are never dies, for death affects only your body, and not you. Because you identify yourself with your body, you believe that you are affected by death. But this is a delusion.

You have accumulated innumerable recollections, impressions, and data concerning the life and death of other people and other beings, and all this is stockpiled in your memory. For you, this enormous mass of subjective impressions and information is reality. This is what you identify yourself with. But because these are only "impressions" in your mind, they could not be that which you really are.

When someone dies who was very close to you, the undeniable pain of loss, which is tied to images and emotions, is very strong. Physically and psychologically, you feel the sadness of losing this person

The powerful images, memories, and impressions surrounding this experience weaken over the course of weeks and months and years after this person's death. The pain and sadness decrease gradually by themselves.

But that which you really are never becomes stronger or weaker, because you are nothing that can be experienced. You are nothing that comes and goes. You never were a body, and you never had a body that could die. Consequently, there is also no memory that could fade with time, for you have never touched or entered space and time.

The superimposed transitory corporeal body

exists only as an impression in consciousness. So, why do you identify yourself with that which you are not? Why do you suffer from that which you never were? You are deathless and formless, radiant divine light!

The waning of the body means leaving behind all one has loved: the people one was close to; nature with its myriad shapes and colors, including magical moments after sunset, when the soft indirect light of the sun paints the evening sky; all sounds; all knowledge. Death is the final destruction of everything known to the mind, the dissolution of all forms.

Never again to see the day, never again to feel the night, never again to laugh, never again to cry, never again to win, never again to lose, never again to be sick, never again to regain health.

Thoughts about the final destruction of physical life and the body, about the decay of one's own body in the earth, or of the body burning up in flames-- these visualizations, packed with emotion, trigger a surge of archaic fears and produce tremendous anxiety. These structures of thought lead one into an unknown, anonymous, and voiceless night.

Will you leave your body, or will the body leave you? Who will leave whom?

Die before you are dead. Then, all superimposed fears, concepts, and images will disappear. And as you were never the body, there will be no one there who could leave you!

INNER REBELLION

Something inside us rebels and protects itself. It does not accept this coercive, overpowering dark force, this death. It wants to live. This inner movement is the natural battle for survival waged by the "I," the feverish search for strategies to persevere in life.

"I don't want to die, at least not now, in this moment." Death installs itself in the mind as the polar opposite of life. It appears to be something that you don't want to know and experience in this moment. Through this antithesis, insecurities and fears of the formless void arise. The mind is fearful of these amorphous depths.

Don't mistake appearances for reality. Appearances carry within themselves their own demise. That which you really are has never appeared.

You sleep in your bed, and in your dreams you travel to distant lands, visit other cultures, navigate oceans, ascend mountains, and cross deserts. But you have never left your bed.

This sequence is analogous to consciousness and the world that reflects itself in consciousness. You have never left that which you really are. You were never active. You have never identified yourself, and have never fulfilled or accomplished anything in the dualistic world.

Stifling fears and insecurity arise due to confused thinking, fantasies, and imaginings. These illusions are given birth through coarse mental substance of material life and are maintained through habitual patterns in the physical world.

What ensues is your compulsion to follow religious dogmas, the repetition of endless prayers and mantras, and the belief that through spiritual practices and techniques you will achieve success.

You look for answers to give meaning to your transitory life on earth. You would like to find out why you are in this world, whether there were previous lives, and whether there will be life for you after your death.

You conjure up or acquire all sorts of strategies from which you believe you will be supported in your efforts to outmaneuver death, because you want to extend your life beyond the grave and are hopeful of an eternal life in paradise. But these are all speculations and concepts, and therefore delusions. Concepts may be helpful to temporarily calm your fears of life and death, but they are worth nothing more.

Images and conceptions of heaven and paradise bestow comfort and impart a feeling of beauty and harmony, but these things have no foundation without the ego, for the one experiencing and the experience are the "I" itself.

After your death, you would like to experience beauty and serenity in paradise. This is where you want to go. But everything that goes, that has, that wants, that wishes for something is the ego, and all strivings are unequivocally the strivings of the ego.

That which you really are is always present. Nothing can exist separately from that which always is. If you do not realize paradise here and now, when will you?

But what and where and how should this paradise actually be? The root of the word paradise comes from the Sanskrit word paradesa, which means "the space over there."

Be aware that that which you really are is free from images. There is no place or location to which you could go, for all places are transitory, and all locations are empty. But you yourself are the placeless here-and-now. You are not something special or specific; you are the essence of everything that is, the most divine of all that is divine.

Death could be called the other side of life, although there is no such thing as another side to life. Death and life are nothing more than fabricated conditions of your apparently dualistic existence.

Pure consciousness never touches the world. It only produces the perceiver and the objects perceived. But it is eternally free from interpretation and identification.

The tragedies you yourself have manufactured within your mind, the cosmic theater of your personal downfall, your own death, will never truly happen, for death relates only to the body, and not to you.

If God had created the world and had himself come into existence, then HE would be transitory, for the creator never exists apart from the creation. Everything that is created and everything that has become something has eventually disappeared again. In this way God would also have met his beginning and his end, and there would be only life and death–no eternity, no Totality.

Just as light does not mingle with shadows, eternity does not mingle with space and time. Eternity is not something that continues on and on. Eternity has nothing to do with life and death. That which belongs to time will never be eternal, and that which is eternal will never belong to time.

Is death that which ends life? Can life itself ever come to an end?

Apart from the "I," the creator of all misunderstandings and an infinite number of concepts, there is no death. The "I" that identifies itself knows death, but you do not.

The problem is not death. The problem is the "I," which is nothing more than a shadow within consciousness, like a mirage in the desert.

Aren't your thoughts of your own death and your hopes for a life after death a betrayal of what you really are?

THE END OF SHADOWS

Imagine that you are standing underneath a huge tree. It is midday in the middle of summer, and when you look down you see the shadow cast by the tree's leaves. But you know that without the sun there would be no shadow and that the sun is always shining, even when it rains or when the sky is covered with thick clouds.

Although the sun, or to be more precise the sunlight, causes shadows to fall on the ground, the sun itself is and remains forever untouched and unmoved by the fleeting scenario of passing shadows.

Just as shadows could never touch the sun, the thought of "I" can never touch the essence, the Totality. The sun itself has never produced a shadow, and the Totality has never walked upon solid ground.

Without the sun, there would be no clouds, no rain, no shadows, and no life on earth. Do you believe that the sun knows anything about the clouds, about the rain, about the shadows that come and go? Do you believe that the sun identifies itself with these phenomena that it affects, but is not? Certainly not!

The sun causes growth and development on the

earth, but the sun's light is and remains uninfluenced by these magnificent processes of growth, maturation, and withering. Through this example you can perhaps have an idea of how the inconceivable, which we call God, through nondoing, does everything.

Eternal nondoing knows no points of contact, no personal interest, no preferences. Although nondoing does everything, there is nothing and no one there to act. Everything happens, although nothing has ever happened.

A good traveler never travels. He follows no path and has no goal. He has never left his universal home.

Is God the cause, the creator of creation, and therefore attached and bound to all things created? Is God responsible for everything that happens on the earth? For all that is good and all that is bad? Did God create heaven and hell, life and death? If so, when?

Shadows arise and disappear upon the earth in the presence of sunshine. Growth, flourishing, and demise occur as well. In sun-filled consciousness the entire world is reflected. Everything here appears to have a body, some stronger, some weaker. But you have never entered or touched these reflecting worlds. The undying never enters the realm of the dying, and the finite never allows itself to be filled with the Infinite.

Creation is an ongoing occurrence, and this occurrence takes place as long as there is an "I" to produce and regulate it.

Sunlight makes objects visible and awakens everything to life. But sunlight is not interested in the objects it makes visible. It does not identify itself with them.

God, "the light of all lights," knows neither life nor death and is not bound within the universe that is reflected in Him.

Without God there would be nothing that exists. But all that exists is not HIM, for HE is neither subject nor object.

For all of creation, for everything that has ever come about or will ever come about, there is no contact point for "the light of all lights," because no identification has ever taken place.

In "the light of all lights" there are no causes and no effects, no place where something could happen. Identification with what comes and goes has never taken place, for the Eternal knows nothing of things of time, and the Infinite nothing of things finite.

Without the Eternal, things of time would have no existence, because the Eternal is the foundation, the essence from which everything in everything exists.

The Eternal and the world of time appear to exist simultaneously and to bear a relation each to the other. But this is not so, as the world of time exists only conceptually.

There are never borders between the manifest and the un-manifest, never separation. Everything is one – you! Within the Totality, the breathless silence of Here and Now, an enormous energy is shining brilliantly, radiating "I"-less divine love. And this grace-filled magnificence, which cannot be conceived or produced, is that which you really are.

Illnesses and the suffering connected to them inhabit the body, but the body is not that which you really are.

When an aggressive disease spreads within the body of a person, a disease that is deemed incurable, the knowledge of this is shocking, a psychological burden that causes tremendous fear and uncertainty.

The incoming information concerning death is registered in the mind, and the consequences are understood. The thinking mind becomes active. The "I" searches in great agitation for possibilities and strategies in order to become healthy and prolong its life in the body. This process is normal. But see that it is the "I" that is intensely occupied with itself, for it is the "I" that has fear, and not the body.

Something fights; something deep within defends itself. Uncontrollable thoughts darken our minds, worries besiege our hearts and souls, and tired eyes look with discouragement upon the transient body within which death dwells.

But at last, when all strivings are surrendered, when hopes of recovery finally fade and dissolve, then the "I" gives up, stops fighting, and stops defending itself.

When this happens, all fears withdraw, and a deep transformation takes place within a person. One is ready to completely surrender one's life to another power, and through this one touches something incomprehensible, something inconceivably deep.

Illnesses and ill-fated events compel people to surrender themselves, but happily, surrendering oneself is possible without painful events and incurable diseases. It requires, however, a wakeful perceptivity that one can deeply see and penetrate through to the origin of that which one really is not.

Awareness yields awakening, and awakening is a breakthrough into an impersonal intensity. This intensity dissolves all indolence, unkindness, and misunderstanding.

The dull energies of personality prevent self-surrender, the breakthrough into the eternal "not-I." The "I" has to go, to give way. But what exactly is this "I"? Where is it, where does it reside in the body? Is it in the head, or does it perhaps spread throughout the entire body? How big is it? Does it allow itself to be located?

Dis-cover what the thinking mind really is, then penetrate the functionality of the "I." Note that just as thoughts arising from the intellect are unreal, the intellect itself is just as unreal. Realize that, before awareness, before the intellect, before thoughts, and before the body, you are!

FRAGMENTS OF LIFE

Your subjective personal life is constructed from a collection of sundry fragments. This assemblage includes set rules, a sustained idea of yourself going forward in life, and a belief in the reliability of these rules and paths.

You live alone and isolated in your personally designed thought-world, this inner realm in which your subjective life is formed and shaped. But, still, you constantly create new ties with other people and hope new relationships will bring fresh opportunities.

You would like to experience peace, silence, happiness, and the realm of timeless infinity. Be conscious that peace, silence, unconditional happiness, and timeless infinity can never be experienced from an "I." These are all attributes of the "not-I," the "not-I" that has absolutely no boundaries.

Transcend your hopes and wants, transcend the free will. The will gains its significance and apparent importance from the intellect, and the intellect is only active within the physical body, which itself exists only as a conceptual appearance in consciousness.

When you penetrate to the origin of the will and destiny, then you transcend both and are happy without a reason to be happy, here and now. Since your birth you have not died, otherwise you would not be here and would not be reading this book at this moment.

When, where, and how you will die in the future . . . you don't know. Everything that you know or believe that you know belongs to the world of concepts and images. You can certainly remember your past, but not your death. You believe the past and future truly exist, and are not aware that these exist merely as superimposed images in consciousness.

The "I" is engrossed in the future, but the future exists only in your thoughts. Therefore, be happy without a future and don't worry about something that doesn't exist. The future is nothing more than a dream dreamt by a dreamer.

You are always now.

For thousands of people every day, physical earthly life comes to an end. Their time in the body has run out. You too are embedded within this process of appearing and disappearing. Be aware of this.

Just as you did not enter the world alone, as a single, individual living being, at a single determined moment, you will also not breathe your last breath at one particular moment, alone, as an individual living being, and leave the world. You do not determine the moment of your birth or the moment of your last breath, for neither your breath nor your life belongs to you.

Cosmic processes are accomplished beyond human will, beyond all thoughts, beyond all stimulation and perception of the senses, and beyond all habits and patterns.

At the threshold of death the brain is swathed in silence, and the world fades. Forceful, unannounced, and inevitable, death flows into the flesh and ends physical existence. Is death the end of all, or is its power limited solely to the physical body? Does death prompt a return of the soul to the ocean of silence?

Death is a unique experience. It elicits various reactions in those who continue living. The death of a person to whom you were close touches you deeply, causing us to delve through emotions and experience pain on the level of the soul. But when someone dies whom you do not know so well, this death moves you very little. You acknowledge this information, and forget it soon afterward.

Although death is the same in both cases, signifying the end of physical life for all living beings, one obviously reacts very differently to these similar phenomena.

This shows how "I"-related this occurrence actually is, and the extent to which one's personal sense of acquiring and letting go, having and losing, mine and yours, is involved.

Apparently the dissolution of shape and form takes place outside or beyond you. You take the incessant continuation of coming and going, the birth and death of living beings, as events separate from yourself. You witness these processes.

You observe something and think about what you have observed, but that which you observed cannot be you. Otherwise you could not observe it.

This shows how you can only observe what you actually are not. You can only observe the things that are fabricated and superimposed within your mind . . . that which you truly are not.

The "I" has experiences, but experiences do not reach that which you really are, for you never entered the realm where an experience is possible. You have never been touched by an experience.

When you become aware that that which you really are was never born, then you will also become aware that you have never done anything within duality.

Throw the illusion of "I am" away and be that which you always are--I AM!

Through your senses you see events and processes that, with the help of remembered images, you assimilate in your brain. The seen, the recognized, and the understood mold that which you see and experience as your life and your world: that which was born, and that which will die.

The body is projected by the intellect, and the intellect has its origin in consciousness, but you are beyond consciousness. Light can never touch a shadow, and the deathless can never touch the dead.

Thought and feeling continually change, but that which you really are is always the same. Thoughts can never pierce through to eternity, and spiritual efforts and exercises also cannot penetrate it. The most they can do is bind one to the transient world, as these activities were conceived by egos, for egos.

The results of will that one can recognize, that infuse and form the subjective view of the world, and the forces of destiny that are formed by them, these "I"-forces, cannot touch the Totality. The will has meaning only in the illusory "I"-world. In the Totality it has none.

Eternity does not exist in diametric opposition to the transient world, and nondoing does not mean that the will is lost, as one could falsely conclude. You are not the one dying, but rather the true awareness of transience. You objectify death, but that which you objectify could not be you, for you are beyond the objectifying and interpreting intellect.

You interpret that which you've seen and heard, and from all the gathered information you have you arrive at the conclusion that you will die. But this is merely an assumption of your "I," which identifies itself with the heard, the seen, and compliant suppositions. Because you identify with the body, you have forgotten who you really are.

At the moment of death, the observer of death cannot be that which dies and is observed. Death first possesses a meaning and reality for you when you place it in relation to something specific, namely, the body. Something does die, fade, and disappear – only that which you really are does not!

How has it come to pass, then, that you believe and are absolutely convinced that your body and all the objects that adorn your life belong to you? Why do you cling so intensely to unreal, temporary phantasms? Why do you lose yourself in a tragedy you yourself have scripted, and why do you confine your soul, which is universal, to the cold secluded abodes of ignorance, unkindness, worry, and pain?

Your true being is like balmy sunlight, which has never been touched by the heavy burdens of the past or by conceptual images of death.

DOES GOD BELONG TO THE WORLD?

Is God all things, in everything, everywhere? Is God everything that is, including you, your thoughts, your feelings, your senses, your mind, and every cell of your physical body?

If that were so, it would mean that when you have a toothache, God also has a toothache, and when you have pain in your stomach, HE also has stomach pains.

If God felt all the pains and suffering of the world, then HE would be continually ill, and HE would constantly writhe from suffering in his heavenly abode. HE would not only be sick, but would also be mortal; he would have a beginning and an end.

To bring God down into the physical world means to restrict God within the brain and the body. God doesn't know the ego, and the ego doesn't know God. Nonetheless, God exists right here, where you are. Be aware of that!

Only a will empty of wishes can realize the changeless. Eternal blossoming is the luminous heart of the universe. This eternal blossoming is beyond existence and nonexistence; it is that which you really are.

The body is temporal, an accumulation of stardust that will disperse and be scattered as stardust once again. But the essence, the foundation of all being, is not dust. The cosmic intelligence that guides molecules and chemical processes is unfathomable, unreachable through thought, beyond understanding and the intellect.

It affects physical existence without being what it affects. It remains untouched by all effects, just as the sun is never touched by the shadows that come and go because of it. This cosmic intelligence is not conceivable for the intellect; it cannot be "grasped." It affects you without being you.

The backdrop upon which the moving exhibition of objects appear and disappear is cosmic intelligence, the original source of all existence. Realize the hidden magnificence within nature, your true inner dwelling!

Beyond the known there is peace. Beyond all religions, prayers, rituals, and mantas, is God. God is a word invented by human beings, but God is beyond all words.

God knows nothing of dualistic polarities in the world, nothing of space and time, nothing of the final deathly hours of mankind. HE is not responsible for the suffering, the worries, the many sicknesses and atrocities of the world. How could HE be? HE never touched the world.

IT is undivided existence, the essence of all that is.

When your conditionings and your many misunderstandings are entirely dissolved, the all-existing is realized.

Death belongs to the world, the thinking mind, the body, and the perceptions of the senses. Death has never touched you, for you are formless, unborn, and deathless.

Your true being is beyond the body and beyond the clustered senses, which are functional instruments of the transitory body.

Death is bound to the senses, to memory, the thinking mind, and the physical form, but the physical manifestations that come and go are not you, for you are here and now.

What is eternal cannot be brought down to the level of the temporal, it cannot be analyzed, because that which is eternal has never entered the mind and never tasted death.

Letting go of uncountable mistaken concepts is Self-understanding, and Self-understanding is what you are.

If God had conceived the world, then that would also mean that God had conceived death. Just as an effect cannot be separated from its cause, a creation cannot exist apart from its creator. Thinking that God conceived the world implies that God has a beginning and an end.

Did God invent mortality, and then retreat speedily into the realm of immortality, into eternity? Why should that which is eternal want to establish that which is mortal? And how would it manage to do that?

Through your identification with the body you experience yourself as mortal and finite. But you yearn to be immortal, to be eternal. Why?

Each person has his own specific worldview, his personal conception of life and the world. But the world one perceives changes continually, and is constantly interpreted anew.

Each moment is different. So transcend that which moments produce, for that which changes constantly cannot be that which you really are. You are the unchangeable. You are only a witness to the ephemeral, the transitory, that which is susceptible to change.

Religious conditioning in the form of prayers, rituals, and righteous tales is indoctrinated into our beings in the earliest years of childhood. These activities and stories belong to the traditional manner of religious upbringing.

Through prayers and deeds of devotion one learns how to build a relationship with God and celestial beings, a relationship with the unknown, the supernatural.

To question these systems and dogmas is to commit a sin. It is explained to us that we have demeaned and denigrated God. Those willing to risk a continued inquiry are told they face severe consequences. One is doomed to purgatorial fires, eternal damnation in the bowels of hell. It was not so long ago that to call religious dogma into question was to be guilty of heresy. One was accused and condemned in the name of God. The resulting punishment was torture and/or execution. One would be burned at the stake or put to death through some other horrible means.

Through strict religious and moral dogmas, humans have been very successful in grafting immense fear onto their souls, and it is through these fears that people have been and continue to be manipulated. These fears aggravate human beings on a very deep level, since, according to the conservative Christian church, we are all sinners, fallen angels, or worse.

Free yourself! Courageously shake out these old, pain-filled stories and fears, for that which you really are has never touched the world.

You pray with your thinking mind, you carry out spiritual exercises, you sing mantras you have learned, and you continue searching internally and externally. There is only one thing that you are not conscious of, namely that the waking state in which you fulfill all your activities and where you formulate your beliefs does not exist at all.

Leave behind the brutal forces of the past, which have produced so many fears and doubts. Discard them entirely and merge your being with supreme silence.

To believe in the sacred teachings, to believe in God, is good. This belief allows stability in our daily lives and helps to cultivate the good in human beings. What would this world be without the sacred writings, without prophets, without avatars, without Buddha or Master Jesus and the other in-numerable saints? Yes, without doubt these are the adornments of God on earth.

Nevertheless, be aware of one thing: The belief in God is a subjective, personal witnessing of a higher power. But the witness cannot be the wit-nessed. Therefore, the belief in God is something abstract, something coming from the one witness-ing, from one who is separate. The belief in God is also not always the same--it is sometimes stronger, at other times weaker, and one can lose the belief in God and become a nonbeliever.

Look deeply and recognize that the nameless, inconceivable, ever-present Here and Now has absolutely nothing to do with belief or religious dogma.

You sit at home in a lounge chair and fall asleep. You dream that you are on a long journey and pass through many continents and countries. You climb mountains, cross oceans, and trek through myriad landscapes. Then you wake up, and in that instant you are aware that you were sitting in your lounge chair at home the entire time, that you never traveled anywhere, that you were only dreaming.

It was no great effort on your part, after having made this long journey, to return to your chair in your living room. How could it be that you were in your lounge chair at home the whole time?

The chair in which you sit and the dream-voyage you experienced in your sleep are nothing but appearances in your consciousness. They have no real existence.

Fatal seedlings that reveal themselves in the "I" as good and bad in the world produce the illusion of an individual life and a life path, which one travels with the sense of existing separately from others. But what always is cannot be reached. It can only be realized. A path exists only for the thinking mind, the intellect.

In awakening, you recognize that you cannot access or come closer to God through rituals or spiritual practices. Quite the opposite: in that way you separate yourself, you turn yourself away from the All-Being. Why?

Each affirming act in this direction creates duality and is a subjective willful act of the ego with clear intention.

As the body is only a thought, a reflection in consciousness, how real and how important can your spiritual practices and efforts be, if God cannot be a goal, and if God cannot be a result for anything but the intellect?

The restless unrelenting activity of the ego causes nothing but unrelenting restlessness, with certain intervals of calm. You experience this calm in certain situations and activities, one of those activities being meditation.

When you meditate, you perform a subjective activity of the ego. Be conscious of this. The ego is making efforts to become not-ego. It practices to control thoughts and to regulate the breath. It names this set of activities "meditation" and the resulting condition the "meditative state."

When you awaken, the activity of the ego dissolves, and meditation naturally arises. God does not practice. The "I" practices. The "I" believes it has lost something or that it could gain something. But the Eternal is always here and now. You cannot desire it; you cannot become it.

That which one controls and regulates becomes uncontrolled and unregulated again. This is how it goes with the practices of the ego.

See through the compulsion of the will and be conscious that the world of the senses is not real. The world projected from the "I" is not you. So what is seeking what?

When you awaken, everything unreal vanishes. The one meditating also vanishes. When you strive to reach the Eternal, you remain separated from it. So be conscious of what you are not! You strive to become what you always are. Your efforts are nothing but a grand illusion.

All activities are only movements in consciousness, images in consciousness, and thus one cannot see these processes as reality.

Within that which never touched the world, there is no compulsion or striving, no wanting or doing, and no intention. The burning force of will rooted in the "I" is, in contrast, constantly active. It incessantly conceives and animates the concepts of becoming, of passing away, of continuity.

All manifestations of life with which you identify yourself are formed from the forces of subjective thinking through which the will expresses itself. They create the foundation for life in society, a model that varies according to modes of cultural and collective configuration.

Don't linger any longer among religious dogmas and cultural mind-sets. Be natural and be silent! In this way you will recognize clearly what you never were.

If you do not completely let go of everything known, the spirit cannot be fresh and uninhibited, and you cannot realize sacred silence.

Be deeply aware of your universal being and within this wakefulness dissolve the illusory intellect. The center from which all illusions and projections arise is not you!

Consciousness is the foundation of all appearing and disappearing, all coming and going, of the perceiver and the things he or she perceives, of all the objects and forms within the visible world and everything in the universe that one can subjectively experience.

Consequently, be aware that that which you really are is before consciousness and the conscious individual. You have never touched the world.

The materials from which you and the world have been created arise, it seems, out of a splendid emptiness. The word emptiness in this case refers to a subtle, sensitive plane of matter, a state in which there is nothing. The mind interprets emptiness as the opposite of fullness and considers these two polarities as real and existing conditions. But the emptiness that can be understood or perceived as emptiness is not the final divine emptiness.

You would like to dig your way out and free yourself from the accumulated suffering of your primal past; you would like to overcome all that is heartless and uncaring in your limited being. In order to fulfill this wish, you search through a myriad of possible solutions.

Once again, read the first words of the previous paragraph. There you will find the root of your primal past, the beginning of your suffering, of your heartlessness and indifference, and of all your other problems. It is the YOU that is born of the "I." Without the "I," there would be no "you." And without "you," the "I" could not be objectified. Your environment, your life issues, and all objects existing within one and the same energy, none of these things could exist independent or separated from the "I."

Your environment and your life issues, and all the objects surrounding you, are subject to change. But that which you really are never changes. You are the unchangeable Here and Now, not the ever-changing "you"!

Because something created exists in your mind, you must follow the logic that there is a creator. But who and how is this creator? All religiously based thoughts and ideas that relate to a creator and creation originate in the brain.

Is God the all-one, beyond creator and creation?

Creator and creation are objectified and interpreted from the standpoint of "I" and "he/she." But the "I" is only a concept, a phenomenon, and you are not that which appears as a separate object--you are wholeness. Because you are not aware of this, you identify yourself with that which you perceive through your senses, and at this point you forget what you really are.

God is not a something, which you achieve or attain, or somewhere you arrive. God does not come from outside or from inside to meet you. God is wholeness, Totality--the Great Secret.

Beyond thought there is no independent object. This applies to what you call the world as well. The problem is that you consider yourself an individual being with a physical form, and you see and understand all other beings from this perspective. But that which you see, understand, and know is not what you really are.

You make efforts on the individual level, to learn and to understand, without the awareness that the one who is learning, the individual who understands, is nothing but an imaginary object, arising just as a mirage appears in the desert.

To recognize untruths as untrue, to see the thinking intellect as the evildoer who causes all your problems, is called awakening.

That which you really are is filled with infinite divine power that spreads itself throughout the entire universe. You are the wakefulness beyond the limited intellect, the vitality pervading all forms, the adornment of the ever-present Spirit. Recognize your Self!

Realize that the vitality permeating the cosmos is an immense universal energy, an ever-present, intelligent power, which you yourself are. You are beyond all depth, you are cosmic boundlessness, the substance of everything substantial, the original foundation of all being, eternal reality.

"Unreal" is what one calls all changeable forms that appear and are transitory. "Real" is what one calls Totality, the unchangeable--God!

Awakening releases an enormous universal energy, a divine inner fire, and this fire brings a great intensity into one's life, an intensity to which the thinking mind and the intellect must surrender. The conceptual image of an "I" and "others" dissolves in this intensity.

Within this fiery intensity, the ego, the sovereign ruler of all fervent passions and potent desires, this powerful king of darkness, must ultimately relinquish his throne. His kingdom vanishes. This is awakening, awakening from a sleep in a sleeping world that has endured for centuries.

Do not observe the activities of the ego. See the light behind them!

WHAT IS SLEEP?

Death is neither your friend nor your enemy. It is that which in reality has never touched you. Death can destroy your body, but not the eminence of your universal presence. You are the liveliness of life, the timelessness within time.

Death relates to the form, the superimposed body image within consciousness, and not to you. If your time on the world stage has run its course, your body will be set down within the earth, or it will be cremated. But what does this matter to you when, in reality, you never were the body?

The flesh is saturated by spirit, but spirit is not flesh.

It is said that sleep is the "little death." This may be so, but God, Spirit, never sleeps. What is sleep, and how do you fall asleep? Just what is happening?

Scientists explain that sleep is brought about through the excretion of the hormone melatonin within the brain. But how do you manage this? With all that you are, all you know, feel, and think, how do you manage to get from the state of being awake to the dream world, or to dreamless sleep? How does this passage come about?

In order to fall asleep, you must abandon all your thoughts, and also the people who live in your home, the family you love, everything you call your own and that you feel belongs to you. Everything in your brain must be discarded, or it is impossible to fall asleep.

In order to sleep, you leave your body and the entire world behind, because there is absolutely nothing you can bring along with you when you go from the waking world into sleep.

This calls forth the question: How real is the waking state, at this moment, as you read these lines, and how real is the dream state you will enter when you leave the waking world?

If "I"-consciousness draws back from the waking world in order to transform itself in other dream worlds, how does this consciousness, which has migrated from the physical body, know the next morning into which body it should return? It could make a mistake, and enter the body of a neighbor . . . but no, this will certainly not happen.

Spirit does not transform, and neither does it shift from one state to another. What appear and disappear are the projected, superimposed states of "I"-consciousness. "I"-consciousness is bound by time. It needs the physical body in order to manifest itself and survive. Spirit Totality is, however, free and untouched by consciousness, free of changes and processes, and free of manifestations.

The waking world and the dream world exist solely as reflections in consciousness. Through their interaction, that which appears and that which fades again generate the illusory concepts of "I was born, and I will die. I am awake, and I will sleep."

The "I" is the foundation for the states of waking and dreaming. This means that all phenomenal objects are dependent on that which "I am." The "I" projects and manifests space and time but is itself not held within space and time. It appears in space and time, as space and time, but space and time and the "I" are only concepts.

Objects are only perceptible to the senses when they manifest and expand within the conceptual sense of space and time connected to the idea "I am."

Objects are evaluated and understood accordingly in relation to this "I am" idea. This shows that nothing separated from "I am" can exist, and that everything that comes and goes is "I am."

So, recognize clearly what you are not.

Can you observe yourself when you sleep? Can you experience, bear witness, and even determine the passage from the waking state to the dream state? Certainly not! In the fraction of a moment, the waking world and with it the thinker and the thoughts, the knower and the known, disappears. This passage is an experience without an experience-er.

The "I" is powerless. It has absolutely no control and no power over sleep, because sleep is a cosmic power that the "I" can neither guide nor control. An unknown higher intelligence takes hold of you, just as it does with all other living beings, gently carrying you into the dream world and deep sleep. This cosmic power is the force that allows physical forms to appear and dissolve again.

Spirit is silence and the substance of life's liveliness, the All-Light.

"I"-consciousness is like a shadow cast by the sun. Shadows are phenomena of sunlight, but sunlight itself is and remains without shadows. You are like the sunlight. You have never touched the physical world, although you appear on the relative level as a body in the world of time and space.

You are Spirit, the universal consciousness inside which the visible world is reflected and manifested. It can only follow then that you yourself are nothing other than life-bestowing Spirit itself, the divine substance of everything that is.

It seems as though hidden desires, primal fears, symbolical urges, and unlived fantasies become activated in the dream world. As in the waking world, these are seen and recognized by a seer, and experienced by an experience-er.

But neither the waking world nor the dream world exists. Both are merely time-conditioned appearances in time-constrained "I"-consciousness. Thus, they are that which you really are not.

Waking states and dream states and the state of deep sleep move interchangeably within consciousness. The waking state and the dream state belong to the transitory world and exist solely as projections in consciousness. Deep sleep is not fundamentally a projection, as within deep sleep the activities of the senses that project the world are inactive. The state of deep sleep differs from waking states and dream states and, in fact, cannot truly be described as a state, because in deep sleep no mental or emotional impulses exist, no movement takes place, and thus no traces of memory are left behind.

Deep sleep is like a harbor into which all sensory activity returns and rests in absolute quiet. The time-constrained "I"-consciousness rests on the lap of deep sleep, whereby there is nothing actively observing in deep sleep that could testify to this.

Deep sleep is the end of the world, for without "I"-consciousness there is no world, as "I"-consciousness is the world itself. Acquired knowledge, the entire mass of seemingly proven facts gained through scientific research and experiments, the entire worldview that the intellect has constructed, all of this is swooped up and swept away completely in a fraction of a second. In deep sleep, the ego is drawn back and laid to rest.

All actions that we have taken in the waking state are based on the concept of "I am": And "I am" is itself the waking world and the dream world. "I am" is the thinker and the world construed from its thoughts.

In the morning when you awaken, you claim that you have slept well or slept poorly. But that which you evaluate is not the sleep itself, but certain conditions that relate to the quality with which you can sense your period of rest, and this you do in a waking state.

You cannot evaluate deep sleep, because in deep sleep the world doesn't exist. Deep sleep is like an invisible current in which the inner waters of the world flow back to a wonderful trustworthy source.

The ego, which celebrates itself and its achievements, and is proud of its transformations, is halted abruptly by sleep. The superficial noise of activity produced by the ego is absorbed in sleep and terminates all memories, including the ideas of life and death.

Oddly, you have no fear of falling asleep, but, yes, you fear death!

It seems that within your psyche there is an invisible drain through which the waking world is siphoned off and the dream world comes to reign. The dreamer in the dream world is the same as in the waking world, only the perceived projections seem distinctly different, based on differing conditions within the space-time dimension.

The waking world and the dream world are two alternating appearances, which reflect themselves in consciousness. After experiencing the waking world, the dreamer and the dreamed all flow back into deep sleep, and this is where the journey of the dreamer ends. It was all a dream.

That which you know and see cannot really be

that which you are, for that which you really are never changes, ever.

That which you observe to be true, because it can be seen and understood as an object, only seems to be true. Be deeply aware of this.

You can also not be what you are looking for, because that which you seek is what you already are. Thought and understanding create and organize this massive Self-betrayal. They produce the concepts of life and death.

The world that is assembled in your brain through complex chemical processes, and then disperses again, is what produces the concept "I am." Through these subjective processes and movements within the brain, a strong feeling of being separated from others, the sense of existing alone and isolated in the world, is produced.

You appear in the world, but you are not from this world, for the true reality lies far beyond the thinking mind.

To consciously discover the entirety of nature as the external realm of God leads you back to the boundless internal realm. Original creative expression in Here and Now, the visible expansive universe, which manifests itself in consciousness as our intimate view of the world, testifies to an immeasurable glory beyond all cosmic commotion.

The evolution of the universe is like a freeze frame on the movement of your thoughts and reflects itself as such in consciousness. The world only exists as perception.

When you fall asleep, you cannot watch yourself, and you cannot objectify the transition from the waking world to the dream world, for these moments of transition complete a kind of "liquefying of life," where the thinking mind cannot be present. All thoughts dissolve, and the individual being flows back to its source in consciousness.

In deep sleep there is no interruption of your true presence, in spite of the absence of one perceiving and of an "I" that understands what it has perceived. The transition from the waking world into the dream world took place within your consciousness, and not within you. Within that which you really are, no such activity has ever taken place, for the waking world and the dream world do not even exist. You are activity-less silence.

CONSCIOUSNESS AND AWARENESS

Are you capable of perceiving the moment you will transition from life to death? Will you be able to understand what is happening to you in the last moments of your earthy existence?

It is not actually the transition from life to death that concerns you and makes you uneasy. Rather, it is the thoughts of what you must leave behind: your body, which was the nearest and most trustworthy companion you had during your entire life, and also your environment, the places and things among which you have lived.

Be aware that that which you leave behind is nothing but an assemblage of thoughts, thoughts of the fleeting appearance of your body with which you have identified yourself with for so many years.

Awakening is another word for being unfettered. Awakening is identification-free awareness that takes place in consciousness. When you awaken, when you are unfettered, you recognize that the phenomenal world is nothing but an appearance in consciousness. Life, death, and the transition from one to the other exist only as ideas in consciousness.

Don't behave as if you are an object. Don't think that you are "something." Disentangle yourself from this illusion; disentangle yourself from that which you really are not!

The lonely, gloomy, and confining power that separates one soul from another dissolves in awakening, and the tremendous yearning to become something evaporates. In deep awakening, the soul merges in silent awe with the Great Silence, joining in the immensity of universal love. Become aware of this splendor, this divine vastness beyond the physical form and beyond the mind, and realize that this is what you are.

You and the cosmic plane are not separate, because the place where you are going is the place you are already present. You are each place, though in reality you are "place-less." In this "place-less-ness" there are no thoughts, for that which you really are is not thoughts. Only an object can be a thought.

Losing your daily consciousness when you experience the transition into sleep causes you no fear, because you are certain that you will awaken in your bed the next morning. But what makes you so sure of this? How do you know?

This certainty is born of conditioned thinking, which is aligned with a sense of continuity and becoming. But this certainty is nothing but an idea, an illusion.

Since your birth, you have fallen asleep thousands of times, and each time you have awoken afterward. Therefore you are convinced of the continuity of your life.

But at some point, at an unplanned moment, death will creep into life and abruptly end this continuity. Just as sleep prevails over your daily consciousness at some severing point, death will triumph and sever this continuity. Death will prevail in your consciousness and bring your physical life to an end.

Death doesn't emerge from some mysterious sphere that exists outside you and then insert itself inside you. It is always there, embedded within your life, from the very first moment of the fertilization of the egg cells in the womb of your mother.

Death is the primordial inseparable companion of life. It is that which ends your outward manifestation in consciousness.

To dissolve this illusory manifestation in consciousness while in the physical earthly body is what one calls liberation or Self-realization.

When this happens, life becomes a delight, filled with indescribable joy. The soul is embraced by a magnificent ever-abiding power and suffused with divine grace.

If you die before you are dead, your being will be illuminated, and you will realize that you have never touched the world.

Events may occur, and your personality may arise, with its wishes, hopes, passions, and worries. But without "I"-consciousness there is no sense of being conscious; without a sense of being conscious there is no cause and no effect to arise from the cause.

The "I"-consciousness is the womb of life and death. Transcend it. If you are aware of the unreality of the "I"-consciousness, then all experiences and the experience-er disappear.

The delight in contact experienced through the senses testifies to something in the depths of our beings, to something supra-personal, to an inner beauty that each conscious living being experiences equally.

Everything one can experience is consciousness. But something such as "your consciousness" or "my consciousness" does not exist, for consciousness is neither a subject nor an object.

The multifarious contents of life, the impressions and information stored in the brain, determine the flow of your life and nourish the illusion of an individual existence.

These impressions are the foundation and substance of the illusionary world. They are also the foundation of your entire communications network in the dense world of material. But the "I" that is communicated is merely a reflection in consciousness, and you are not that!

It is truly a miracle that a nonphysical energy cloaks itself in a material body and in this way makes the subtle entities of the world visible and accessible to experience. A still greater miracle is that this physical manifestation transforms within this physical world of appearances.

Through the experiences that you have stored in your memory, you shape your life and determine your goals. Through the myriad images of your journey through life, you come to know moments of pleasure, excitement, passion, monotony, and bitter disappointment. Along your life's path you feel compelled to test out many things.

These activities and subjects are nothing more than a diversity of decorations for the "I"-consciousness. Therefore, be aware that these fascinations and life issues are hollow and have no real existence. That which you really are is free of issues, will-driven activity, and destiny.

Do the contents of memory really reside in the cells of the physical brain? Or is the brain only an instrument, a switchboard for the memory? Spirit and consciousness are connected to the brain. This shows itself in awareness.

Recognize that in everything you do each day, including the most complex acts that you carry out, you are not even conscious that you are doing them. You perform your tasks more out of your unconsciousness than your consciousness, out of the stored memories and previous experiences that have lodged themselves in the unconscious. To a large degree these unconscious energies navigate and determine what you think, what you feel, and how you act.

In the different regions and throughout the complex switchboards within the brain, scores of millions of impulses and impressions are processed. They adjoin themselves to that which you experience as the perceptible interpretable world of the senses.

Without consciousness, you would not be aware of the world of the senses you have accumulated in your brain, and your brain could not think about itself.

Spirit could be defined philosophically as the intelligence that guides all neurological processes and makes them possible. But Spirit is much more. It is not only the foundation of everything that is, it is everything that is.

The impulses that become active in the diverse regions of the brain due to sensory activity are processed as material information. The mechanisms, the complex processes that assemble the world of the senses in the brain, are identical in the brains of all human beings.

But do not forget that you are not the brain in your head. You are that which is aware of it. You are neither the knower of something nor the something that is known.

What makes one person different from another besides outer appearance, gender, and cultural heritage are the inconceivably enormous masses of miscellaneous information that are stored in the memory and unconscious. The floods of information acquired and remembered in the brain compose the entire knowledge of each particular person, and you identify yourself with this knowledge and define yourself according to what you know.

As a being that "knows," you sense yourself as an individual and perceive your world from this perspective. You interpret and construct this world anew according to what previous knowledge you have, and you are also convinced that the space you inhabit belongs only to you and to no one else.

How strange! Spirit defines itself through consciousness by means of the projected physical body that appears in consciousness, and then binds and loses itself in entitlements and delusions.

The more specialized one's knowledge has become and the better one can remember and express that knowledge, the greater one's reputation in society grows. This is because one can demonstrate that one has learned much, and is therefore a "knower."

It is impossible to live on the earth without knowledge. One is therefore constantly endeavoring, through learning and assimilating new fields of study, to extend, expand, or amend the contents in one's storehouse of memory.

To know a great deal seems attractive, because it allows one a superior or more advantageous standing in society. In the conceptual construct of society in which we live, the expression, "knowledge is power" is validated to a certain degree.

Yes, you can study many things and know many things. But you cannot learn or know that which you really are. The Timeless recoils from the sphere of material knowledge, from the narrow, Self-constraining thought world.

Through religious knowledge and highly cultivated language, the illusion that one can come nearer to God, to the Eternal, is produced. But one cannot elevate oneself to God's level with thoughts, knowledge, and activity, nor can one enter God's kingdom, as one might imagine or as one would dearly hope.

Spiritual practices, rituals, and prayers awaken deep, beautiful, religious feelings, but these feelings that are produced can soon fade or disappear. It seems that if one mechanically repeats these activities, one can avoid the fading and loss of these religious feelings.

Indeed, that which is produced will dissolve again. The thing produced arises from the striving of the subjective activity of the will belonging to the relative "I"-consciousness.

So don't arouse anything. That which you really are is beyond existence and nonexistence, beyond subjective feelings and beliefs or nonbeliefs.

The Timeless, the Eternal, is not something instilled, not something that exists with you and in you in the world. Just as light does not get involved with shadows, the Timeless doesn't get involved with time. There is no common ground between the two, but without light there could be no shadow.

The idea that there is a path from the mortal to the immortal is an illusion that is produced from the thought "I am." Consciousness assumes the identity of a certain form and thereby forgets its true nature.

Knowledge introduces the images you retain of the world. The known is the world. But since these images and your knowledge also change constantly, you never know exactly what and how this world actually is.

Depending on your frame of mind, the world at times appears beautiful. At other times it is revolting. Sometimes it feels heavenly, other times like hell. But these states of mind are not what you really are. Mental commotion, the subjective projections of life and death, are never able to touch or penetrate the Great Silence.

Unity is of a contrary nature. It is completely unfamiliar for the "I"-consciousness.

When an object is seen as an object, there must be a subject differentiated from the object. But neither the object nor the subject really exists--you are awareness.

The wanderer never left home, for neither he nor the home really exists. To realize this is Self-realization.

THE POWER OF KNOWLEDGE

The known is projected through what is conscious, and the known is what is conscious. This is how the discernible image of one who experiences and what is experienced arise in awareness.

An enormous tumult of activity is set in motion through this dynamic, which unfolds in our consciousness as an engrossing current of life, full of storms and swirling shifts, soaring heights and abysmal depths.

The observer influences what he observes, whereby the observed is not something determinable, substantial, or objective, since it changes due to its dependence on the observer. The observer produces his reality and continually influences it. This is why there is no such thing as an objective reality.

That which you observe, understand, and assess as reality is a product of "I"-consciousness.

"I"-consciousness is the creator of this vehement, uncontrollable, and unpredictable current, with its innumerable good and not-so-good thoughts and emotions. This current, this driving force, attempts to restrain, to control, and to conquer, but each and every willful effort solidifies and strengthens the illusory image of being an individual, a personality. That which you believe yourself to be is certainly not that which you really are.

The "I" is the producer and at the same time also the victim of its own production, of its own projection. The "I" appears on the great stage of the world theater, but neither the theater nor the producer nor the actor playing out his roll on the stage really exists.

But here, in the abyss of time, is where violence and hate make their home, where humans driven by their will are at work. Here, instruments of power are cultivated, instruments originating in the "I." One of these instruments is, as we have already seen, knowledge.

Those who know more stand higher on the plane of knowledge than those who know less. In the history of mankind, entire classes of society were controlled, manipulated, suppressed, and prohibited access to resources of knowledge.

Secret agencies, religious institutions, and other factions have consciously applied this weapon of knowledge, and still do so today. In this way, the "I" is the cause of all corruption or is, in fact, corruption itself.

Knowledge Has Many Faces

Through the course of centuries an incredible accumulation of knowledge has taken place. The known has been ceaselessly expanded, amended, and updated.

Knowledge, ripened through experience, has allowed humanity to push open the door of the Technical Age. Amazing innovations have been imagined and produced to serve humanity, and the achievements have been truly monumental. In the fields of medicine, physics, and biochemistry, in the worldwide expansion of telecommunications, in aviation, architecture, and many more areas, humanity has, in the last sixty years, accomplished a quantum leap.

Collective structures throughout the world are changing at a blistering pace. Social problems, the many wars, world hunger, increasing shortages of sanitary drinking water, and the many complex environmental problems that are brought about by these shifts of structures compel humanity to think of new alternatives and abandon the ways of old.

In order to orient in a new way, it is indeed necessary that the old egocentric models of thought are seen through and let go of. Only in this way will humans be able to meet the needs of the vast, interconnected global community.

This is easier to say than to do. The conditioned modalities of thinking we humans have developed are tightly constrained. Programmed, conditioned thought and the entirety of accumulated knowledge are at their limits.

It appears that the accessible resources of knowledge, the general sum of knowledge, and the egocentric thought structures connected to our knowledge are not sufficient to solve the problems we will be facing in the near future. The materialistic intellect has reached the threshold of its capacity. The ego, with its perverse, destructive facilities, is being tempered.

But to be a human being is something magnificent. Be deeply aware of this! To be a human being means to be wide awake, responsible, and aware of the world one lives in, for the world is exactly what you are.

Be fully in the world, and be fully not of this world!

Awakening brings an end to all fatalism and fanaticism and erases all restricted and illusory models of thought. Awakening is not a religious escape from the world, and not an ascendance to some spiritual plane. It is very sound and stable: both feet on the ground and our mind in Eternity, in the spiritual universe.

Look deeply within yourself and recognize that acquired knowledge is restricted within the thought-world of time and space. Only there is it important, only there is it effective and of value. Be aware that that which you really are is "no-knowledge." You cannot know "you."

You are in the world, but not from this world. You are wholeness, Totality.

Everything you know is not you, and you cannot become that which you do not know. Knowledge and "becoming" exist only as superimposed images in consciousness, and as they are illusory, they do not touch you. Knowledge and thought only play such an important role in your life because you have not yet made your departure from them.

Is death and everything you know about death merely that which you have retained in your memory?

A small child does not fear life, nor does it fear death. It lives in the moment. A grown human being, on the other hand, has experienced many sad events, losing numerous loved ones to death. Painful memories of leaving and loss etch deep impressions in the memory. Therefore, one perceives death as a kind of unconscious emptiness, as cold, void of light, as the darkness where all activities, feelings, and thoughts come to an end.

The "I" wants to retract itself from these uncomfortable thoughts and repudiate the thought of its own death. The "I" fears nothing more than its own end. This is why it is so concerned with mortality and immortality.

The thinking mind tried to think the unthinkable, to imagine the unimaginable. The "I" has the desire and hope for a prolongation of life after death. It wants continuity.

Thought concerns itself with abstract images. The intellect tries to extract the best possibilities in each situation, based on what it has, what it has read, and what it has seen. The "I" wants to live on and secure its domain, but the thought "I am" is the birth of time, the true birth of life and death.

"I am" identifies itself with that which "I am" imagines. Through this illusory act, "I am" takes itself captive. "I am" is the prison cell, the prisoner, and the prison guard, all in one. That is the tragedy of "I am."

You believe you are something. But you never were that "something." You believe you have gone through situations and experiences, even though, within that which you really are, nothing has ever occurred.

Through belief, hope, prayer, and various rituals, the "I" attempts to organize its life after death. When this life is over, it hopes to take on a more spiritualized form, one where all worries have disappeared, where it can continue to exist in a heaven satiated with light.

The "I"-consciousness is not aware that it is doing this, that it itself has no real existence. Heavens and hells, life and death, they only exist for the "I"-consciousness because it itself is the cause and effect of these images.

Be aware that there was never a world outside of thought. Life and death are no more than interpretations of processes within the world, interpretations of an apparent beginning and an apparent end of life and the world. When you awaken, you are aware that you were never the body and never the mind.

Consciousness, within which the world reflects itself, seems to lose itself in "becoming" conscious and identifying with the reflection of the image "I am." Through this delusion, the nonephemeral becomes ephemeral, and what is timeless is bound to time.

But you are neither form nor formlessness, neither mortal nor immortal. You are Totality.

Consciousness identified believes in the experiential world of the senses; in life, death, and reincarnation; in good and bad in the world. Oh yes, all this is right there for the "I," because the "I" is nothing else but this.

Through your spiritual search, you seem to want to prove to yourself that you really are there. The moment in which you read these lines is what you really are, for beyond this moment, nothing else exists.

Your search for the unity you've yearned for is your problem, because you never were anything other than what you seek. You identify yourself falsely with that which you are not. That is why you have started seeking.

The world and the entire universe exist within the Totality, and therefore they really do exist. They exist because of their relation to the inseparable unity of all.

One calls the world and the perceptible universe unreal and illusory because they appear, fade, and change constantly. Totality is called Totality because it is not subject to change--it is the essence of everything that is.

Death is a theme that has always concerned human beings. Religions point to a world that transcends death, where life continues after death, in other worlds, in other spheres.

The hallmark of the Christian faith is the crucifixion, death, and resurrection of Jesus Christ. Whether the resurrection really took place as it is described in the Bible is doubted by science. One assumes that the story of the resurrection is allegorical, to be viewed as a metaphor, because there is no sound scientific proof of the physical return to life of Jesus Christ.

There is likewise no scientific proof of the existence of God, but there is also no proof that HE doesn't exist.

Some believe that there is God, and that Jesus rose from the dead. Others are convinced that neither God nor resurrection exists. One cannot know what God is, in just the same way that one cannot know what God is not.

Why does the universe exist, and why is it the way it is? Why did conditions, resources, and possibilities that permit human life appear on one small planet in a relatively small galaxy?

Approximately 13.5 billion years ago the universe was born. But what was happening before this "big bang," and why did this massive explosion come about?

These are questions that are not easily answered, not by science, and not by religion.

Nietzsche enraged the God-believing masses with his pronouncement, "God is dead." This statement also strengthened the arguments of the atheists. Nevertheless, for those within organized religions, there is no doubt that God exists.

These two models of belief divide humanity. What, then, should one believe? What can one believe?

The foundation of everything, absolute potential, could be called "God." But manifestation is only introduced and made perceptible through the concept of "I am."

The "I am"-concept is the subjective projection and the universe one perceives. The perceiver and the perceived reflect themselves in consciousness, and consciousness is a reflex within absolute potential, in that which you really are.

As you are always Here and Now, you can certainly not die. Creation and destruction are only for the "I," and not for that which you really are. To realize this could perhaps be called "resurrection."

Love is that which does not interfere. That is why it is called "divine" or "God."

THE DANCE OF DEATH IN LIFE

One's own death is a thought that arises in consciousness, and this surfacing prompts a profound confrontation with the meaning of this word. You connect the word death with an event that you are certain will take place at some point in time. You are certain that this event will be the end of your physical existence.

The emotionally charged thought-energy that infuses the word death works its way deeply into "I"-consciousness. Through your senses, you have experienced how other beings have fared when death has put an end to their lives. You do not know the exact time of your death, but you know that at some particular point death will enter your life and put an end to your physical existence in the world.

In this world, nothing is certain other than the fact that, at some point, you must leave this physical world. The subject of "death" compels you to contemplate the end of your life in the world and the end of your physical body.

You philosophize about death, read about it in holy scriptures, or suppress this delicate subject matter entirely, out of apprehension and fear. But death does not contemplate, nor does it suppress. It has nothing to do with philosophy or religion. Death is the end of all thinking and all knowing. It obliterates the physical world of the senses.

Because you cannot remember your future, this ultimate departure from this world that you foresee leaves a black hole in your brain. You don't know when or how death will end your life. But this should not be too disconcerting, for that which you really are has never touched this superimposed world. The "I am," the body-concept, exists solely as an image in consciousness.

Religions offer consolation and conviction to provide the faithful with strength to better endure their eventual departure from this world. But with this consolation and conviction, a perspective of a life in a spiritual world after death is also instilled in the believers, possibly a heaven, or perhaps a hell.

Desires, passions, and longings, it is said, lead the soul to the underworld, to hell. Virtue, kindness, and loyalty to a faith allow the soul to enter heaven. This may be correct, but the source and cause of all subjective actions are purely concepts, as is the subjective individual who acts.

When this is discerned, and the unreality of these conceptual images is penetrated, the question then arises, "If the 'I' is lacking, who are heaven and hell actually for?"

Heaven and hell exist only in relation to the "I," the creator of all superimpositions. The "I" identifies with the superimposed inventions and images and survives in constant interaction with these forces.

Be aware that you are beyond interactions and beyond heaven and hell. You are Here and Now, an impersonal ocean without shores, a flowing stream of powerful energy without a source.

Religions use the images of heaven and hell as an instrument to instill subservience in their believers. The images are dark and invoke fear and foreboding. Through their unbounded fears, humans have allowed themselves to be successfully manipulated and restricted. We are told that the good will be rewarded, and the bad will be punished.

Since, according to the Christian religion, all people are essentially sinners, no one can be truly certain, in the end, if they are good enough to enter heaven. This uncertainty remains until the very end. Perhaps one does finally land in hell.

Before one leaves the world, in the last stage of physical existence, one says farewell to the people one loves, to the places that have been significant, where one has felt at home, and perhaps also to the body, which one must finally leave behind. Sometimes these farewells are not possible, and this is a fact we are all aware of.

Therefore, be awake and comprehend this point: These words are about your clear, thorough farewell from farewells, and your death before death, now!

Can you, in this very moment, bid farewell to

the entire conditioning and magnetic forces, to the powerful, conceptually formed, deeply imprinted storyline of your life, which your being forms in your body?

Can you absolve yourself from thoughts, from the concept of your impending death and that which comes afterward? Can you emancipate yourself from the conceptual idea of "I am the body"?

Be aware that the moment of death will be now, not yesterday or tomorrow!

Whatever you have experienced in your life, an experience-er was necessary, one who had the experience. The same goes for the life in the hereafter. Life before death is life after death. But life before death and life after death both exist merely as conceptual images in consciousness.

You will not find silence and you will not find infinite splendor in life before death, and also not in life after death. You are that which you are in the infinite Here and Now!

A gentle stream of universal energy embraces everything that exists, and everything that exists is this divine stream of energy. There are actually no souls, only the "soul-filled." No one has ever left a body. This only appears to happen for the one perceiving, who has been blinded and deluded by the things he or she has perceived.

An event occurs, perhaps, and perhaps a person exists, who believes or disbelieves, who also has desires, needs, and hopes. But without consciousness there would be no one there who could experience something, and therefore no causes and no effects.

Without "I"-consciousness you would not be conscious that you exist as a person and a body. Thus, without the "I," the question of a life after death does not arise.

This shows that the "I"-consciousness is bound to life and death, is indeed life and death. See through the functionality of the ego! This penetration can dissolve it.

The imaginative dreaming one experiences is born with thoughts of "I am." They are your subjectively produced world. The "I" and the thoughts are not separate occurrences. They belong together, are united, and represent exactly that which, in reality, you are not.

From the projected "I," the projected "you" is derived. It then appears in time and space, which are the foundation for all suffering and all confusion. Through this subjective movement in consciousness, a separation in original consciousness takes place, a deformation of your natural presence in Here and Now. That which you really are has never moved and never touched the world of suffering.

Due to thoughts of "I," you become an object. The object itself is even so a limited, time-constricted phenomenon, and nothing more. That which you perceive through your senses, that which appears and disappears, the environment in which you live, and all objects within it, could never exist without the "I."

The individual as such has no exclusive independent existence and is, within the Totality, nonexistent. Outside of Totality, nothing has ever existed.

Within original consciousness there are no desires, no hopes, no needs, and no suffering. Penetrate the murky illusion of the "I" and banish it from your being. Merge with the Eternal, with that which is free of shadows, with that which you really are.

Thought within the field of the mind is in constant movement, is ceaselessly active. Locked within the narrow restricted holdings of the thinking intellect is the chamber where one also obtains and retains an understanding of God.

The thinking mind strives feverishly to escape these constraints and yearns to discover the boundless spiritual vastness beyond thought. But the yearning and striving can only be based on adopted concepts and images, which are founded on restricted modes of thinking devised by others.

The intellect clings vehemently to its stored knowledge, to what it has learned and understood. To take leave of the known and the understood is very unappealing and creates apprehension. One is afraid of forgetting it all. The will resists this farewell, this forgetting, and begins to struggle. This struggle creates more fear. Fear fears nothing more than fear itself.

The more you know, the more you are aware that you know very little, or nothing. To realize this means wisdom. It also means freedom from the burden of the known.

Knowledge is neither good nor bad. It must be differentiated. The sage Shankara said of knowledge, "Due to knowledge, men stay clear of snakes and thorns. Due to their ignorance, some run into them. So you see what importance knowledge has."

The painful fact of passing away, passing from this world, is a thought that accompanies human beings with each breath they take. This uncontrollable, unchangeable fact hangs around the neck of humans like a lead weight. Because we are destined to be banished at the hour of our death, fear, suffering, anxiety, and misery ensue.

Be aware that you, in reality, have never come from anywhere, and you will never go anywhere.

You are here and believe you were somewhere else, although this "somewhere" never existed. There is no place to which you could go, for that which you really are has no place.

From the time you were born until today, you have not experienced your physical death. Otherwise you could not be reading this book right now.

Be aware right now: you, your environment, this book, and all objects in space exist in the same consciousness. Nothing can exist independently of the universal Here and Now, from Totality, that which you really are!

Objects appear and vanish again, but you are beyond all objects. You are that which never touched the world. You are conscious of the world without being the world.

Departing finally from "body-object" is not your departure. How could it be, when you are eternally unborn? What hurts is not death itself, but the thoughts about the loss of the body and of the world one experiences with the senses.

Awakening allows dis-identification from the confinement of the body, and swallows up the straying, rambling illusory thoughts of death, just as ink is absorbed by blotting paper.

You suffer and feel sorrow for your loss, for your departure from something other than what you, yourself are. But you cannot, of course, be sad about yourself, about what you really are, since you are deathless and unborn.

Neither the ego nor the intellect truly exists. Temporary shifting forms appear and fade away, but the origin has no form and no characteristics. Penetrate the temporary as temporary, see the false as false. In this deep awareness, that which wants to seek and find dies, and the way and the goal die as well.

The thinking mind looks for eternity in corporeal images, but it lingers in the muck of slavish conceptuality, because the one seeking and the thing being sought are nothing more than constructs, reflections in consciousness.

You know the world, but does the world know you? You know your body, but does your body know you? You were born without an intellectual storehouse of knowledge, and your intellectual theoretical knowledge will be of no use at the hour of your death.

That which you have perceived with your senses externally through the course of your life is what you know about your body and about death. The intellect consists of a bundle of thoughts, and with them you can formulate anything, except what you really are.

That which you know relates exclusively to the external, the temporary, the mortal. But death does not take place outside you. It takes place within you, with you, directly.

Because death occurs directly in the Here and Now, you cannot perceive it, nor can you objectify it. Your subjective knowledge comes only from the death of others. You know nothing of your own death, other than that you will die. Here and Now cannot die. In death, only the overlaying images dissolve.

"I"-consciousness has no genuine foundation. It arises and vanishes again. Life and death are like this as well. If you penetrate the emptiness of the intellect and the emptiness of "I"-consciousness, the idea of "I am the body" is extinguished.

In actuality, the person you believe yourself to be does not exist, and this means that the experiences you believe you have had, and the waking state in which the "I" lives, do not truly exist. Be aware, you are that which is prior to any manifestation of anything.

The stockpile of information in the brain and the emotional energies bound up with it are the nourishment upon which the shadows of death mature and thrive. Over the years, they appear to solidify themselves in your being. Death exists solely as the polar opposite, as the counter-interpretation of that which you call life.

In vague ignorance and empty-heartedness, "I"-consciousness stares out at the dull material world and identifies itself with what it sees. While looking around, it contemplates its own earthly life and also plans its life after death.

The thinking intellect thinks about itself, but it remains trapped within the closet of time. It is not aware that it itself is nothing more than a relative appearance in consciousness. Eternity does not allow itself to be contemplated or planned, nor can it be desired or understood.

Can the Eternal, that which never touched the world, die? Or is dying related only to the subjective image of "I," to the superimposed world that appears and fades away in mental consciousness?

The world exists because it is perceived. It is the perceived itself. Because perceived images are falsely interpreted within the intellect as individual beings, personalities, and objects, the illusion of "I," "you," and "others" arises, of "mine" and "yours."

Life and death are creations of the subjective "I." They are that which you really are not.

NO OBJECT

When you lie in bed tonight and fall asleep, this transition toward the sleep state, this flow out of the waking world and into the dream world, will not take place outside of you. But where will it take place?

You seem to draw yourself out of your worldly wakeful body and return to a dream body and a dream world. This happens without your will or your nonwill. It just happens.

Dream consciousness expresses itself through a dream body. Your body in the waking state expresses itself through a physical body. Both bodies are appearances that come and go. Both are instruments that support and transport various states of consciousness.

The driving force that allows both of these worlds and their instruments of support to appear is universal consciousness. The two worlds of appearances, the waking world and the dream world, reflect themselves as fleeting shadow impressions within universal consciousness. But they are not universal consciousness itself.

Be aware that universal consciousness is that which you really are!

You are not the dreamed-up personality that appears in its various life scenarios. You are beyond the one dreaming and all that is dreamed.

True freedom and liberation cannot be achieved through any kind of striving or practice, for the one who appears and all that appears, the one who dreams and all that one dreams, are illusions.

Spiritual practices, techniques, and methods have been conceived by egos to satisfy egos. The ego proudly retains the concepts and alternatives it learns. The ego, the will to act, is the activity and the actor, "I, myself." How real, then, can these methods be? And who are they for?

Together, the object of recognition and the object that recognizes generate the compulsion to act. But that which acts is illusory. It does not really exist. Awakening transcends the recognized object and the object that recognizes and dissolves the will to act.

Spiritual strivings reveal themselves ultimately as vain decrees of the ego. The ego has one desire over all others, one goal: to control, to dominate, to reign supreme. The ego has successfully learned to command and control itself and, oddly, it calls these efforts "spiritual"!

Emancipate yourself from these vain desires and veer yourself toward timeless peace, the Great Silence. In the Totality, nothing has ever happened.

Let the divine force of universal consciousness take over and guide your being. For you, there is nothing to do.

When this is realized, the word devotion takes on a new depth, a new meaning. Devotion arouses pure intuition, intuition that has nothing to do with conceptual thought and practice. Intuition is direct awareness of that which you really are not, and the realization of that which always is.

States of consciousness can only be defined and understood through their contents, the identifications and subjective impressions one perceives. Identification with what fills consciousness illustrates the functionality of "I"-consciousness. Without a seer there is nothing to see. Without someone experiencing, there is nothing to experience.

One's superimposed mental constructs of activity are nothing but processes and motions of the dynamic will, which belongs to the ego. Where there is a will, there is only a way--a way that in reality doesn't exist.

You don't have a way, and you are not a way. You are pure awareness. To be aware of the relativity and the emptiness of what fills consciousness produces dis-identification. Dis-identification is awakening.

In deep sleep, sensory consciousness rests within itself. Here, there is neither a dreamer nor something dreamed, no seer who sees something, no one there to have an experience, no something, no "I," no "you," and no "others." But nevertheless, you are!

Deep sleep is not a state of unconsciousness. It is

the absence of sensory activity. Sensory consciousness finds itself in a temporary state of rest and is not aware of itself or its state. In the waking state, as in a dream state, the sense of being something or someone is present. In deep sleep, this sense is not there.

The waking world and the dream world seem connected with deep sleep, but that which you really are is beyond deep sleep, beyond the dream world and the waking world, beyond all interactions and beyond consciousness.

Life comes and goes, but you are always here. Where else but here could you be?

In the waking state, in the dream state, and in deep sleep, Totality, the All-One, is absent, because Totality is the essence of consciousness. The world of the senses reflects itself in consciousness, in the dream world, and in the waking world.

Deep sleep is the place where the sensory world temporarily retreats and thoughts of "I" are disempowered. But deep sleep is not a condition or state, not a specific place. It cannot be objectified. For this reason it is also known as "the little death."

That which you really are is beyond consciousness. You are Totality!

Consciousness is the source of all perceptible forms, including yours. You do not exist separately from consciousness, where you appear and leave again. And although the one who experiences the "I" is absent in deep sleep, deep sleep is nothing other than consciousness.

Awakening also dissolves that which produces moments. Through this, one's wandering thoughts and one's wandering hopes are also dispelled. They melt away like ice in the sunshine. The illusory idea of being a body also evaporates.

All contents of the mind, all ideas and all information that is saved and stored in the brain as memory, are purely conceptual. So, that which you believe yourself to be is certainly not that which you really are.

Consciousness is the foundation and the background upon which the gigantic torrent of information gathered over a lifetime is built. The world arrives and departs again upon this superimposed foundation.

The world that is visible and perceptible is assembled in the brain and only exists as a superimposition in consciousness. Yet Totality is eternally free and untouched by superimpositions, because the experience of "I am" exists merely as a concept in consciousness, and the world exists only in thought.

At the cinema, the movie screen upon which dramatic flood or damaged by those catastrophes. It is just like this with universal consciousness.

Film images of catastrophes can be intense, emotional, and absorbing for the audience to the point that one forgets that one is in a movie theater. Dramatic moments are true and real for the cinemagoer, to the point that you forget that you are only watching a film, that the images you are observing are only alternating reflections of light projected onto a white screen.

You inhabit the world that you perceive through the senses, and live from the power of the images and processes that are collected and conceived in the brain. These images are fascinating and hypnotizing. Within this subjective intensity of experience you completely forget that what you have experienced is only a set of images in consciousness.

As long as you see yourself and define yourself as a body-intellect-being, and identify yourself with the seen and the understood, you remain an object that comes and goes, that lives and dies.

Turn inward and discover that you are life-giving universal consciousness itself within manifestation--the foundation upon which everything explicable and inexplicable exists. You are the foundation of all thoughts and feelings, but you are not what is thought nor what is felt.

Discover what you really are and be aware that, in truth, you are beyond consciousness, beyond the manifested and the un-manifested. You are Totality.

Within "I"-consciousness the idea of a long journey on earth arises. One has reached many frontiers and gone down countless paths. Suddenly the wanderer awakens and is aware that the wanderer as well as the journey was illusory. The person who went from here to there never existed.

To recognize this allows a radical breakthrough,

a true revelation. All restrictions, all the hardened forms that the "I" has created, collapse. Silence is revealed. All horizons disappear.

The world "beyond" is in this world, and this world is in the world "beyond." They condition each other and are two sides of the same coin within your brain. You have never traversed into or contacted either of these illusionary, transitory worlds. Your true home is Totality, and you have never left it.

Both worlds, "this side" and "the beyond," are ephemeral. They are worlds in which individual patterns vibrate, worlds in which the ego expands and can experience itself within consciousness.

The individual celebrates itself within the relative time-space dimension. But the conceptual individual that experiences life and death is nothing but an overlaying of consciousness.

The principal dynamic of the ego is the will. It is this that constructs and maintains the subjective cerebral world. Mental constructs with their wobbly scenarios take on hundreds of shapes, names, and forms. To the intellect these appearances are all real, although in truth they are not. They are like shadows moving under the sun, a constant changing of costumes sponsored and goaded on by the ego-will.

Things of finality and finiteness can never have an effect where constructs do not exist. The limited can never recognize and realize the Eternal. The finite has no knowledge of infinity. The infinity of the universe is beyond the thinking mind.

As long as the mind is active, confusion reigns. If the thinking mind is transcended, that which you really are is illuminated.

Mental concepts, identifications, and ideas are all bound to the physical form and dependent on it. But all identifications are nothing but ideas, delusions, and therefore not what you really are.

Awaken and "dis-identify" yourself. "Dis-cover" your mighty origin from which you never departed. How could you anyhow? You are eternally formless, unborn, and unbecoming, never arriving, never going, always here, always now!

Everything which was, was merely a dream. Names and forms were nothing but imaginings, nothing but reflections in consciousness. The long journey of your thought ends here and now.

So, where is "the beyond"? How can something beyond you and separate from you exist? Who goes where? Who is the one who has the experience of "the beyond"? If this "one" is absent, the experience would not even be possible.

Where do experiences take place? Where do they come from?

With everything you have achieved through spiritual practices, with everything you have been told, and with everything you have read, you have a tremendous amount of conditioning. For this reason, it is difficult for you to realize what you are not.

The will that loves to plan functions only within its limited radius of activity. Herein, it tries to accomplish its short-lived goals. Everyday thoughts enslave the body and constantly compel it to take action.

The ego uses the world as a means to exert power, to satisfy lustful desires and momentary cravings. It is always anxious to apply the knowledge it has accumulated as a tool to control everything in the external world. It wants to get what it thinks it needs, and to claim those things as its own property.

Thus it is very clear that the ego is the source of all corruption. Indeed, it is corruption itself. Through activity, the ego can feel itself and understand itself.

The subjective idea of a beginning and an end to life relates exclusively to the form, the corporeal. But you were never that.

Birth is the fuel of life. If it arises, death follows. Birth and death are that which the "I" is, but "I," in reality, does not exist.

Where were you before you were born? Discover that which never dies. Then you will be at peace.

The more the soul is illumined through insight, the clearer it can discern the relative field of "I"-consciousness where life and death are played out.

When you have this insight, you become deeply aware of what you really are not and resolutely overcome your ingrained habits. The primal crust of your being cracks open and disintegrates into nothing. You were never anything other than nothing! In this way the being returns to essential being and is the Great Silence.

The "I" stimulates, strengthens, and supports the conceptual world. The "I" lives and experiences nothing but its own projections.

Within these subjectively stimulated ideas, a kind of mental magnetic detention center is installed, where the "I" is trapped in its own imaginary conceptual images of "this side" and "the beyond."

As long as you live on the outskirts of reality and identify yourself with rigid forms, you will not be able to inhabit the illuminated, boundless continent that is your true home, to flow into that eternal ocean of light.

One can understand on the level of "I" that heaven and hell do actually exist. They express the exact internal character, the most primal mode and manner of the ego. "The beyond" is like an echo of "this world," within which the game of good versus bad resounds.

Your countless mental constructs falsify your actual clear and pure presence. Egocentric forces restrict you in dull routines and cycles of endless desires, wishes, and hopes. You are the motive and the mechanism of destiny's forces, which confine the soul in worlds that are only half-conscious.

Through your thoughts of an individual being, an invisible but massive building is erected, and you live trapped within its walls. In this solidified form of thinking and seeing you experience yourself. You are conscious of yourself as "I"-consciousness.

These thoughts, and everything they arouse and

incite, are activities of the dream "I," which lives in its own dream world.

Break through this narrow viewpoint and do not let yourself be blinded any longer. Be aware of how the habitual outer stratums of consciousness determine the movement of earthly things, things that never touch you in pure awareness. Immortality or mortality relate only to the outer form and exist solely as ideas in consciousness.

In pure awareness the long journey of the soul through time comes to an end. It enters an immense light and becomes that which it enters.

The ocean of eternity does not come into contact with the adventurer who wanders through the world. It knows no intentions and has no geographic configuration, commitment, or plan. Not a trace of darkness is to be found within it, and yet nothing can exist independently of it.

The ocean of eternity and the wonderful organic systems of the world which make formal life possible are not separate. They are one.

But human thought has the audacity to imagine itself the arbitrator and umpire of truth, and in this way it creates separation. Uncountable misunderstandings are thereby produced, which are then seen and understood as true, although they are not.

Thought plays such a big role in your life only because you never transcended thought, and you fear that without thought, you will not be able to function.

The thinker as well as the thoughts he has appear important for the completion of necessary activities in everyday life. But when it is clear that the thinker can only act in relation to relative knowledge that has been stored in the brain, then the thought instrument itself becomes relative.

Totality cannot be an object of thought and recognition. Only the transitory can be an object of thought and recognition.

Thought produces an expanding conceptual world that is full of doubt and insecurity. But you are not that which is thinking, nor that which is thought!

Don't practice in order to control or curb your thoughts. The ego would just love that, because in that way it can willfully strengthen itself.

Be aware that, in reality, you are neither the body nor its functions, and you are not the relative world of appearances that reflects itself in consciousness. You were never a body, and never had a body, because you have never touched the world.

Life expresses itself through the body. The body doesn't express itself through life. The body is the instrument through which life shines.

The sun also shines without the moon, but the moon would be completely in the dark without sunlight. It is just like this with the essence and the body. Essence, universal consciousness, also shines without the body, but the body does not shine without essence, without universal consciousness.

Realize this before you are dead. Your being will then be filled with a sweet and serene lightness, abundant with that which you really are.

WHO WANTS TO BE REINCARNATED?

A large segment of humanity believes that after death their lives will continue in "the beyond." There are numerous religious, mystical, and esoteric views on this topic.

One assumes that, after death, the subjective sensory constructions that produce the forces of destiny will guide and carry the soul with invisible wings to its determined place--either up above to a paradisiacal world, or down below to a dark and dismal underworld.

In the Christian doctrine, it is proclaimed that the uncorrupted soul will live eternally in paradise, while the soul that has transgressed will remain in purgatory or hell.

The Buddhist doctrine teaches that one will at some point be reincarnated, in some cases with the body of an animal.

In the Christian belief system one presumes that only one life on the earth is allowed. In the Eastern doctrines one has many lives, one succeeding the other.

This may all be true. But these experiences require one who experiences them, one who lives out this life or these lives. It requires an "I"-conscious-ness, an ego.

Awareness of consciousness is the awareness prior to consciousness. Therefore, awareness tran-scends the one experiencing and the experience and all that one is conscious of.

From the viewpoint of science, there is not one irre-futable proof of life after death or of the existence of God. In contrast, millions of people are convinced that God exists and that life goes on after death.

The brain constructs its own truths and realities. It also constructs life after death, and perhaps it constructs God as well.

If you are without attachments, these questions will never arise, because, in reality, you are univer-sal, formless, indestructible, nameless, and unborn.

The word incarnation stems from the Latin "cari-us," meaning "flesh," and "incarnare," meaning "becoming flesh" or "becoming human."

In the Bible, in the Gospel of John, it is said that the son of God becomes flesh, Jesus Christ. In the traditions of India, the avatars, divine incarnations, have distinguished and represented the old reli-gious traditions until this day.

Seen in this way, all humans are souls that have become flesh. Otherwise, they would not be here on earth. You also would not be here.

But where did all these billions of souls come from? Where were they before they were born?

Where were you before you were born? Did you come from an invisible world and enter this visible world? Will you then return to this invisible world when you have been liberated from the flesh, like all the other souls? Where do you come from, and where are you going?

The cells that are in a waking state experience the world through the psychosomatic organism, through the senses. This world is reflected in consciousness and interpreted by the thinking mind. In this way consciousness seems to become conscious of itself. Is the breathing flesh-body the place where consciousness, through being cognizant of itself, becomes conscious?

The essence, the magnificent light of eternity, bundles itself in consciousness through the body and is revealed through it. But essence is never touched, never tainted by experiences and identification with the senses, which all come and go within consciousness. So don't strain yourself in an effort to become free. Your sense of being trapped is only your imagination.

An intensity of perceptions transports the soul into a kind of hypnotic state, but the soul is not conscious of it. Here, the objectifying object and the objectified object arise, which means nothing less than breakage and separation from universal, all-encompassing love. In this way, the immortal becomes mortal, the boundless is bound, and the Eternal has an end. For the personalized "I," death seems real. For the depersonalized "not-I," it doesn't.

Awakening means to be aware of what one really is not, and to realize what one really is, namely the nameless, formless, unborn Here and Now, the eternal Self!

Surging waves of peace and love flow through the soul and the body when this is truly realized. Peace and happiness are never based on something external, for peace and happiness are not an object and do not dwell in objects.

Birth might be seen as a loving gesture of universal consciousness. The conscious body could be perceived as a ray of light arising from the soul in which it lives. But neither the body nor the soul can exist separately from Spirit, from God.

An individual being has never left essential being. How could it? The individual being exists singly as a temporary overlay on essential being. The individual being itself only arises through erroneous identity. This erroneous identity is the foundation of suffering and the deep abyss of loneliness.

The sensory images of the planet Earth and her immeasurable splendor--the ancient trees, the mountains, the silent vastness--are all what you perceive externally with your the eyes. And they are also what you are inside--consciousness!

Penetrate, see beyond the cupboards and closets of the restricted, see all the way through and be aware of the light of the universal sun within. It is that which you really are.

Transcend the body and the thinking mind--if

not now, when? Human life is like the dream of a dreamer. Both are conceptual and are not, in fact, that which you really are.

"I"-consciousness, which is itself both the objectified object and the objectifying object, constructs the foundation upon which the concepts of life and death thrive and flourish. The soul discerns this information in consciousness.

Through the activity of the senses and the resulting contact with the outside world, the fictional "I"-consciousness installs and positions itself. Here the soul submerges, without being aware of it, into the mire of time and mortality, and thus enchains itself in illusory mechanical routines and processes.

The powers that build up the mental world also build the road toward demise and death. Heaven and hell, "this world" and "the beyond," are fully inhabited within this complex, mentally constructed world. They are the causes and the effects of the mental being, of "I"-consciousness.

The "I" clings to its longings and hopes. But it is never able to comprehend the inner supremacy of pure presence. It can't, because that which really is, is the "not-I."

The resilient "I" stretches out its expansive will and, within the context of its particular beliefs, begins a celestial experiment: it plans its life after death.

The soul, encased within the loneliness self-induced by this menacing, mentally created "I," forgets the grandeur of its ever-present nature, and through this superimposed "I" is deposed to do battle with death. And in this battle against death, the "I" is able to experience a sense of its own continuity, a sense of its personal life and approaching death. The thinking mind pushes against the walls of the body, upon the borders of its own externalized boundaries.

Within the lackluster mental world, the luminous glow of pure being--the radiance of Totality--is neither perceptible nor comprehensible. The meaningless depths of the "I" and its predicaments identify only with the overriding doubts, with the callousness and confusion that belong to it.

But ultimately, dissatisfaction and the feeling of restriction induce human beings to turn around, to turn inward, and this is good.

When the turnaround is complete and the "I" gradually fades, then the immortal, all-embracing divine power reveals itself. It carries the soul back home and fuses it with the eternal Here and Now. This river does not flow into the ocean. Its course runs back to its original source.

DO WE LIVE ON INFINITELY,
OR ETERNALLY?

One believes that the soul lives on after death in a spiritual world and that it will at some point be born again. This would mean that the soul is living through a process of successive existences that is not interrupted by the physical death of the body.

Seen in this way, the soul would live on infinitely. The expansive designs drafted by the mind unveil the fictive concepts of a tomorrow and a future. The "I" would dearly love to believe this.

All occurrences in time (which are actually what rebirths are) are like imperceptible phases within the expansive designs of the will and the intellect. This gives rise to the question: what is it that is actually reborn?

Under what conditions do you live without your body in the other world? How long must you stay there before you are reborn again? Can you think in "the beyond," and is there also an ordered life to follow? Are there activities or events there that change or determine our destiny?

When you live on in "the beyond," will your experiences, feelings, and perceptions be similar to the ones you have now in a physical body? Is there a vocation awaiting you in "the beyond"? Does one have the sense of "I am alive" there, or will you think, "I am dead"?

Becoming is always accompanied by diminishing, by dying. This is exactly what reincarnation is. Rebirth is only the continuation of dying. The uncountable multilayered processes set in motion by the mind that shape your everyday life are nothing but concepts, images, and ideas.

You continuously busy yourself here, striving to find harmony and balance in the muddle of becoming and diminishing, but you have certainly grasped long ago that it really isn't working out.

This isn't working out because concepts, images, and ideas are nothing but subjective mental constructs, reflections in consciousness, which in themselves are insubstantial, empty, and hollow, like bubbles of air on the surface of the water.

Oddly, you continue to identify yourself with these empty constructs and hold tightly to many illusory ideas. Moreover, you are ready to vehemently defend these things that do not actually exist.

In awakening, you are aware that neither "this world" nor "the beyond" nor reincarnation could be real. Reality cannot be where temporary things, places, or worlds exist.

Leave all concepts behind and realize that which you really are!

You believe or imagine that you were born in the past and are now in the present, although, from a deeper perspective, there can be no present, since the present never holds still. Rather, the perceived present always seems to be shifting, progressing toward an unknown future.

You observe time as something separate from yourself, as something you must live through and endure. But this is a delusion, for neither the experienced object nor the object that experiences truly exists.

Totality is everything. It permeates everything. So the idea of having one's own individual life is an illusion. Beyond thought there is nothing and no one there, no one called "I," "you," "he," "she," or "they" who could know or experience anything.

As long as you see and experience yourself as "something," you are deluded, hypnotized by the power of your subjective self-manufactured scenarios and ideas. Here, you and only you live, alone in your own egocentric universe.

This is why you are trapped, trapped within yourself, trapped by yourself. You are the prison cell, the prisoner, and the prison guard as well.

Birth, life, death, and reincarnation are like mirages in the desert. They are nothing but false and delusive images in consciousness.

How does reincarnation occur? A tree is planted. It grows and slowly develops. The stem rises higher, becomes broader and stronger. More and more branches are produced, some big, some small. Many corollary branches appear as well. When the tree has matured, it blossoms, and countless fruits are produced. These fruits carry the seeds for new trees of a similar type.

It is the same with people. One is born, slowly grows up, becomes big and strong, and carries the seed for future growth. In the case of human beings this seed is a compelling compilation of distinctive experiences, ideas, images, desires, dependencies, strategies, and concepts.

The quintessence of this seed produces the personality that a person feels, lives out, and portrays in this world. When the physical body is old and used up, the moment of death arrives, the moment where one apparently leaves the body. The inner-dwelling invisible seed, the entire potential of the inner "I"-person, contains many intense forces that are resolutely determined to develop and be expressed.

The character of a person, that which one calls personality, is invisible, hidden within the flesh. Therefore no one knows exactly who and how another thinking, feeling person is. The inner person uses the physical body, which one sees and senses as "my body," as an instrument through which that which is internal can be expressed externally and made visible. One feels like an inhabitant of one's own body-house.

Within this inner and outer dynamic we each experience the world we ourselves have produced. The internal produces the external, and the external produces the internal. The internal conditions the external, and the external conditions the internal. They are dependent on each other and never exist apart from one another.

Thus, right from the beginning of thinking life, a fatal seed is sown that bonds the twins of the ostensibly good and the ostensibly bad on earth. The conceptual images of origination, flowering, withering, and dying rob the soul of its ageless innocence.

Your life on the earth is formed according to what is seen in your inner mental state. This state of knowledge forms your everyday life, from thought to thought, and experiences all the highs and lows along the way. The theatrical stage of the mentally construed universe guarantees the prolongation of the will, the ego.

Mortality and immortality relate exclusively to outer form. So then emancipate yourself from these ideas, because you have never touched the world.

Your physical body is a picture with which you intensely identify yourself, and although it changes constantly over days, months, and years, you still persist in proclaiming, "That is me."

The "I" is aligned with and adjusted to the manifested, to outer forms, shapes, and appearances. But this could not be any other way. The "I" itself is what objectifies as well as being the objectified object.

Thus, the "I" cannot awaken and be liberated through any kind of practices or efforts, for the "I" itself is only a passing phenomenon.

Awakening happens!

BEYOND THOUGHTS

Strong identification with figurative images is a powerful force, one not to be underestimated. For it is precisely this force from which, at the time of leaving the body, a new body is projected, like the dream body experienced in sleep. It is born out of "I am" thoughts and is nothing other than "I am." This ethereal body is a kind of copy, like the negative of a photo taken of a person standing in a landscape.

But everything that has an origin will also have its demise. This means that death continues also in "the beyond." It means that to be reincarnated is nothing other than to be appointed again for death.

Therefore, die before you are dead, and be aware that birth and death relate only to the body and not to you!

When you awaken, your heart will be touched and filled by an unfathomable delight. This delight tears down the lonely limitations of a restricted life.

The soul awakens to the gentle dawn of internal light, emerging from a sleep that has lasted thousands of years. The journey through time has come to an end. As long as the soul has not awakened, it remains trapped in the sphere of night, wandering from life to life, from death to death.

If, at the moment of your death, in the inner sphere of night, stripped of your physical wrappings, the internal fate-determining forces continue to be active and vibrate, then the entire conceptual life vibrates on in another sphere, in a nonphysical sphere one calls "the beyond." Or so it appears.

However this may be, "the beyond" cannot exist separately from "this world," and without ego, there is neither one nor the other.

Life in "the beyond" is, then, a life beyond the physical body, a life in an ethereal body. But the processes of the will and the fabrication of conceptual images continue. This means that the field in which the entire past vibrates doesn't die when one leaves the physical body. It continues to vibrate. In this way, false images of physicality are reanimated and sustained, bringing with them the concepts of becoming and dying.

The seemingly solid physical body on "this side" and the seemingly ethereal body in "the beyond" are both dream bodies, nothing but appearances in consciousness.

Any identification with the physical body creates the sphere of night. It is the sphere of night itself.

Be aware that you are eternally free from the enclosures of time, and free from any physical bindings. You have never entered the sphere of night.

You are in reality formless, body-less, deathless, the "not-I."

When you awaken, the earth-born voices quiet down, and the Land of Silence is revealed. An undying power embraces the soul and transforms it into the "uni-soul." Everything that makes you special disappears. All particularities disseminate. There is no one and nothing present other than awareness itself.

As long as the "I"-seed is there, the world is there. As long as the world is there, there is growth and decay, suffering and joy, and the sphere of night.

As we have already seen, the "I"-forces behave similarly to the growth of a new tree. A huge tree develops out of one tiny seed. The entire image, the complete structure of the mature tree, is stored and latent within the seed. As soon as it is sown in the ground, it awakens and begins to grow and mature into a tree.

Invisible information below the ground transforms into a large visible tree expanding above the planet. Mother Earth makes this possible.

Nine months after an egg cell is fertilized in the uterus of a female body, a small new physical body enters the world. Over years this body develops to maturity. All external events occur due to an internal seed, and the mass of all events forms external life, the outer world of appearances.

When a person leaves the body in death, the internal forces that produce fateful events construct a new body out of the foundation blocks within the seed. This happens in "this world" as well as in "the beyond."

Where worlds appear and disappear, physical forms are reflected. Where physical forms appear, death and reincarnation exist.

Each person lives within the limits of his or her own nature, until death and entry into the limitlessness of Spirit. Die internally now, before you are dead!

The "I," which in itself is illusory, uses the physical body as its instrument for expressing, recognizing, and defining itself. This happens in "this world" and in "the beyond," because the ego represents the foundation of both these worlds. This is the sphere of night where the "I" in its dull ignorance is caught in the cobwebs of the brain.

The thought and feeling of "I live" and "I will die" give form and shape to this sphere of night, this nucleus of the ego. They are the "I"-forces that guarantee that you will live on and that you will die. Death lives on.

"This side" and "the beyond" appear to truly exist for the "I." For the "not-I," they don't. Dream appearances reflect themselves in consciousness, so there is not something like an autonomous, individual being that exists separated from Totality.

The biography of the planet Earth seems to reveal an evolutionary diagram, to render a story. But the purpose of this evolutionary plan, the theme of the story, is unknown. You are in the world, but you don't know why.

In order to justify and validate your existence in the world, you invent uncountable concepts of a psychological, philosophical, or religious nature.

"I" is looking for the meaning of its being. This is meaningless. Be aware that that which you really are never allows itself to be contemplated or understood.

When you realize what you really are, then everything that is not real falls away, including the meaningless search of the "I" for the meaning of life.

If there is a universal destiny for humanity, it is certainly not one that can be subjectively studied, planned, or intellectually understood.

It seems an all-encompassing universal consciousness is the intelligence that determines the means and ends in the processes of all that exists. This universal "not-I" force, which is everything that is, is what you really are.

"I"-consciousness, the thinking mind, is born and will die. You won't.

You do not know how many bodies born of the "I" and carrying seeds for a future have come and gone successively over thousands of years. You don't know how many millenniums your soul, due to heartlessness, misunderstandings, and rock-hard egocentrism, has been imprisoned in the chasm of life and death.

That which you know is what you are not, and that which you believe you know is also not you.

The image you have of yourself is the memory of what you believe yourself to be.

The vivacious beauty of ever-presence can be perceived and experienced through the senses, but this ever-present, illuminated splendor is not born of the "I." It reflects the everlasting magnificence of Totality.

You were never what comes and goes. You are that which is eternal and everlasting.

Death is embedded in each rebirth. The end of life is rooted in each life. The harvest will show exactly what was in the seed when it was planted. This is how the law of cause and effect works within space and time.

The fatal forces of becoming and declining are the cause of all suffering. See through them!

The merciless will, the instrument of cause and effect, drives the soul from death to death. But the soul intuits its eternal ancestry in the higher light of reason. This intuitive recognition is expressed as a deep longing for transcendence.

Uncountable inclinations, desires, wishes, and experiences, all accumulated knowledge, and all the different denominations of faith; all are in the brain, in the unconscious, stored as vital information. You can call upon this multitude of stockpiled information in the subconscious, and you can give it new life by contemplating and evaluating it again.

In this way previous thoughts, ideas, notions, philosophies, and concepts are renewed and expanded, and then sink back into the subconscious. Later, through some outer impulse, through stimulation of the senses, they will be called up from the subconscious, altered again from their previous form in some way. You use this mechanism to put together what you call your daily life. This is how you experience it.

You identify yourself with this world that has been put together in the brain, and you are convinced that that with which you identify yourself really exists. But you restrict yourself unconsciously with this identification. You bind yourself within the webbings of death, and you darken the soul.

It seems apparent to you that you and the world were created. But, in actuality, these are only images originating with the concept of "I am."

Collective aptitudes and attitudes arise due to these dynamic egomaniacal forces. Examples include collective fear, collective hate, collective anxiety, and the collective belief in death. These constantly alternating inner battlefields strengthen the "I"-feeling. On these ugly plains humans become cruel, unscrupulous, and coldhearted.

In this way a human being lives in his or her own darkness, in "this world" and "the beyond," in these two worlds that are nothing other than the dynamic structure within which the ego expresses itself. These coercing "I"-powers compel the soul into a state of superficiality, trapping it in the mire of time.

The will to exist is the force that holds the random fragments of an illusory life together, unconsciously constraining them within the confines of time.

When the powers sustaining the search for meaning are awakened, the ego proceeds to the belief in an expanded life, hoping thereby for supremacy and glorification of its power-oriented domain.

The "I" wants to do something, to develop, to cultivate itself. This will is also the foundation for the exercise of spiritual practices and techniques. But techniques, rituals, and spiritual practices are of absolutely no use in realizing the Totality. They serve only to increase the number of concepts upon which they are construed.

Be aware that there was never a way through mortality leading to immortality, and never a way leading from time into the Timeless.

Because the borders of the "I"-being are demarcated and unyielding, the ego realizes at some point quite painfully that its domain is illusory.

The individual aspect becomes exhausted at its own boundaries of perceiving. It is not capable of seeing through its own self-woven veil. The will also becomes tired, because human powers can never facilitate access to divine Totality.

You were never the body that appears and fades away on the relative plane. You have never existed in "this world" or in "the beyond." You are the egoless Here and the egoless Now.

Spirit is uncreated. Thought has never touched spirit, for thought is nothing but the thinking mind, which is nothing but ego. The thinker and that which is thought appear and disappear. Spirit is eternal.

Thought is your loyal companion. Therefore you trust your thoughts, thoughts that seem to be able to make dreams come true. But thought cannot recede from the rigid world, for it itself is the cause of its own effects.

You can change yourself, but Spirit is unchangeable.

To forget what you really are is death. So awaken--if not now, then when?

The dynamic information stored in the subconscious and related   inner-dwelling energies determine the atmosphere in which you live and how you express yourself. You use these forces, driven and shaped by the will, to plan your life, and you behave according to this goal-oriented dynamic. These subjective forces, these dispositions, influence and determine your life. They are your life, and also your death.

"Dis-positions" create passions, and passions enchain the soul. It is the "dis-position" that is born again. Dispositions are nothing but the ego. It is not Mr. or Mrs. X that will be born again. Only the disposed "I"-seed that has not been liberated continues to vibrate in "the beyond."

According to the interior prearranged information within the seed-energies, the soul is forced back into the physical body. This is nothing mystical or romantic. It is the expression of a compelled, confused, incarcerated soul.

In this way the seed plants itself and insures its continuity. Because the "I"-core in "this world" and the one in "the beyond" are essentially one and the same, all the information stemming from this core with its multitude of vibrating states is also the same.

There are basic states and moods that emanate from the "I"-core, and those states are multiplied, cultivated, and developed with additional aspects and components by new input.

The thirst for physical life that originates in the identification with the physical body is the determining force that projects a body again in "the beyond," an ethereal body. But here again the law of cause and effect is at work. This means that what appears will and must disappear.

The body in "this world" and the body in "the beyond" are both nothing but reflections, nothing but dream images in consciousness.

What appears and disappears can, in any case, not be what you really are, for you are not transitory. You are eternal.

Strip yourself of the burden of opposition. Overcome the tumult of time. Merge with the gaze of the most beautiful of all, the most magnificent of all, and realize what you really are.

As long as "I" exists, the soul is chained to time and continues its dream of life, death, and rebirth within a mortal body.

It seems that in previous lives, and also in this one, there were opportunities when one could succeed in changing or improving one's life, or one could make one's lot worse. These possibilities exist and have existed in each moment. But all subjective activity, seen correctly, is nothing but self-amusement at the edge of one's own boundaries, one's own captivity.

The life path drawn up in the brain is plagued with fantasy and is full of confusion, anxiety, and dull concepts. Beneath the weight of this shadowy cerebral sheath, the radiant soul is suffering.

The so-called "bad" in you is like a lead ball tied to your left foot, and the so-called "good" in you is like a golden ball tied to your right foot. The good and the bad are two sides of the "I." Whatever you do, "I" is always the cause and "I" is always the effect. That which acts has effects, but in the finite, where cause and effect function, no limitlessness, no eternity exists.

See through the trivial game of the "I." See through these false images and useless concepts and realize what you really are!

The illusion of life and death fades gradually with awakening. The sower of seeds and the seeds sown are burned away by the divine power of grace, which is awakening itself.

The radiance of the soul ultimately rids itself of the rough scaffolding of time and emerges in the glory of eternal light, finally at home again!

HOW AND WHAT?

What do I have to do to be or become Totality? How do I achieve Self-realization? The actual problem, if there really is one, would be this "what" and "how."

As long as you see Self-realization as a goal, as something that you would at some point like to experience and understand, you will remain confused and caught in concepts.

Self-realization is not a goal. It is the realization of that which you really are.

The "I," which itself is unreal, believes that it can achieve Self-realization at some point. The ego understands the body as itself but tries, at the same time, to recognize its origin. With this seeking, the ego hopes to cultivate the Self. But reality lies beyond the mind, beyond seeking and the sought.

When the "I" becomes exhausted and surrenders, then the unfathomable depths of the "not-I" open up. You then go beyond the broadest borders of your inner individual human being and submerge in that, where no word or thought has ever penetrated.

Internally, you attempt to find out who you actually are. Along with this seeking, mystical feelings arise within you. But seeking is an act of the mind, a movement that spins in circles and always returns to its starting point, specifically the "I."

Seeking is thinking. But what and who thinks? And why? That which you really are has never thought, for you are the eternal uncreated "not-I."

Thus, the thinker and thoughts are also what you are not. You are neither the objectifying object nor the objectified object.

Thinking produces thoughts of life, death, and rebirth. Thinking produces this vicious cycle within time.

The mind looks for solutions, ways to escape this cycle, but it never succeeds, because the "I" itself is the strategic master and the strategy. The "I" is the prisoner, the prison, and the cause of imprisonment. The "I" tries everything it can to outsmart itself, but it remains stuck within its own tightly structured limits.

The soul surges backward, back to the ocean of peace and contentment, while the "I," as if hypnotized, stares into memory and perceives the delusive images there. It sees what seems to be an individual life with a seemingly individual past, and identifies itself with it.

The heartbeat of the Eternal, the splendid gown of universal love, is not to be found in today, yesterday, or tomorrow, because the Eternal is eternal--eternally free from the fuel of the changeable, of the ephemeral.

Pumped full of subjective images and ideas, the "I" gallops forward, toward its own future, a future that, in reality, doesn't exist and never did.

Yesterday and tomorrow exist only because there is a today, but today, yesterday, and tomorrow are only ideas, nothing but fleeting thoughts. Today seems to be the axis upon which yesterday and tomorrow turn. But this entire movement is purely illusion.

Emancipate your perspective from this slavish viewpoint and awaken--if not now, then when?

The search for one's own attachment in the realm of causes and reasons requires time, while awareness is free of time. In pure awareness, the questions of "how," "what," and "why" dissolve.

LIFE IS ONE

Divine power, which is enormous, impersonal, and unlimited, is repressed and mistreated by the personal will. Divine light is twisted around, beaten, and restricted alas to hard labor in the construction and maintenance of the self-serving ego world.

In the subjective egomaniacal world, only the ego emerges. The "I" produces the fantasy-filled portrayal of world events, nourishes it, and sustains it triumphantly.

In the rigid environment within which the "I" vibrates and exists, the soul is not capable of being aware of its formless delightful sweetness. The will, which produces miserable cravings and gloomy scenarios, prevents this.

Through willful action, the Divine becomes dreadful. The Eternal becomes time-conditioned. The "not-I" becomes the "I."

On the level of the "I" you are the grand architect and builder of your own destiny. You go on living in the present, which is the reward of your past. Your present reflects your past, and your past is your present.

But you don't know how far back and how

broadly the past is reflected within the "I." You also don't know when this reflection, your "I," began its journey through time.

Does this reflection extend to past lives? If so, how many? When did the present become the past? How did the "not-I" become the "I"? And why?

These are questions the ego asks. In its curiosity, it wants to know more about itself. It wants to experience its origin. But this ego-screening is not true being. You are being, not screening. You are that which never touched the world and was never touched by the world.

Don't look back, and don't look ahead. BE!

You determine in which direction you move along your subjective life's path. Through a willful, conceptually driven process, the feeling of living from one moment to another arises. You live on.

The grandly conceived panoramas of the self-scripted life-theater with its intellectual entitlements always have the same ending: internal breakdowns and utter devastation. Breakdown and devastation are usually very painful. But through such experiences the relation of many things is clarified. The transient and the superficial become more obvious.

Recognize the source from which the world and your life originate. Recognize that which causes you to perceive, understand, and experience the world the way you do.

The restrictive force of the objectifying object

and the objectified object allows the ideas of life and death to appear. How is it when this force, produced from yesterday and today, is not there? How is it when the objectifying object and the objectified object don't exist anymore?

Trapped within the fleeting world, the soul journeys to the frontiers of time, restricted each step of the way by the plentiful delusions that cling to it. It wanders restlessly through the two valleys of death, the illusory landscape of "this world" and the illusory "beyond."

You live within this subjective universe, inhabiting the structures you yourself have built, and you develop a compatible lifestyle. Your mind submits itself to intelligible, graspable energies and flings itself into the subjective transitory world of thought, where the will plays the lead actor. Here, you crave pictorial images and their conceptual content. You crave hopes, desires, and passions.

You are not aware that it is consciousness that induces this cosmic panorama in all its monstrous proportion and presents it as truth and reality in your cerebral awareness. You are not aware that this formidable cosmos is dependent on you witnessing it, on you confirming it.

Without the perceiving object and the perceived object there is no world, because the perceiving object as well as the perceived object are themselves the perceived and interpreted world of the senses.

Because you are conscious, the conscious manifestations of the world are real to you. If you were not conscious, there would be no world. Thus, the foundation of the universe is consciousness. Through physical manifestation, consciousness seems to be consciousness that is conscious of itself. But that which your really are is beyond the conscious world. "I" is the conscious world; "not-I" is Totality.

The internal and the external are transitory. The universal, nonpersonal is eternal and unchanging-- that which you really are.

TO WHOM DOES LIFE BELONG?

The "I," the actor, considers itself an illustrious lord, but its limited domain is the domain of death.

The subjective force of imagination that is active in the temperamental "I"-sector spurs humans on. We are excited about our self-created worlds, where we can operate effectively. But this subjective world is nothing but a dead end within Totality.

The force of imagination can never penetrate or contact the eternal depths of the not-"I." The Timeless never mingles with the time-conditioned, and the Immortal never mingles with the mortal.

The problems and projections produced by the "I" will be relocated from an apparently visible place to an apparently invisible place, from "this world" to "the beyond."

The invisible internal steps out of the physical body and out of "this world" and the entry into another world "beyond" are a journey of the "I." This journey is based on the results of dead half-truths, on inflamed energies emerging from the mire of "I"-centeredness.

The problems piled up on the physical plane of the "I" will be seamlessly sent on from "here" and carried over to "the beyond," where they will be experienced again in different conditions.

If you believe or hope that you can slip away from these old illusory energies after leaving the physical body, you are making a terrible mistake. An incessant compelling force, the law of cause and effect, drives the deluded and confused soul relentlessly forward, through the conceptual world in "this world" and "beyond." The dull forces of the "I" materialize themselves and unveil subjective panoramas in "the beyond." The "I"-human being experiences itself living in the throng of its own bright and blackened impressions and emotions. This happens in "this world" as well as in "the beyond," since both worlds are the "I" itself.

"I" is the foundation for these unreal worlds, which are nothing but appearances in consciousness. The form-impeded soul wanders through its inner world, and what the "I" has sown the "I" will harvest, as the causes can never be separated from the effects.

Therefore, discover that which never dies, and be deathlessly happy!

EVERYTHING IS OK

In the field of empirical science there is a hypothesis that relates to every organic living thing. It goes: "Life creates conditions that contribute to its preservation. Organisms influence their physical-chemical environment to their own benefit."

In other words, life creates the world that it needs. From this viewpoint the cosmos would be a super-organism, and the planet Earth would be a living being.

The brain is responsible for pronounced feelings such as love, hate, envy, sadness, and happiness. The brain allows you to think, hope, doubt, believe, and forgive. But what exactly takes place inside this thousand-gram mass of fat and tissue is still to a large extent unknown. Whether the brain is capable of thinking about itself and can decipher and comprehend its own functioning process is an open question.

We are far from really understanding ourselves on the physical level. There are no ultimate answers relating to our physical being. There are only new and more profound questions.

But those who awaken transcend the questioner and the question.

To seek God is like asking the way to one's house while already standing inside it. You complain because each person gives you different directions to follow.

You think you are here and God is somewhere else. And you must seek Him and find Him. Through your efforts you hope at some point to enter eternity.

See through this profound delusion and realize that the world has never touched you.

All is well, really! Everything is in order. Transcend that which creates disorder and be in peace, in the silence beyond perceptible silence!

Love all human beings, love all living beings-- when your heart is full of love, you will not suffer anymore and you will realize Totality.

The divine power of love is without beginning and without end. It is that which you really are!

Don't be afraid,

I AM HERE!

For more information on books, talks and darshans
by Mario Mantese/Master M
www.mariomantese.com

Other books in English
by Mario Mantese/Master M

In the Land of Silence
This autobiographical novel depicts
his fateful encounter with a spiritual master
in the Himalayas.
ISBN 978-3-8423-9166-6

Puplisher: www.bod.de/www.bod.ch

In Touch with a Universal Master
This unusual biography portrays the life
and unbound spiritual work of this Master.
He is a man of miracles.
ISBN 978-3-7699-0626-4

Puplisher: www.dreieichen.com

*Online shopping with payment processing
through PayPal and credit cards is available*

CPSIA information can be obtained at www.ICGtesting.com
Printed in the USA
LVOW04s2359250115

424309LV00022B/317/P

9 783732 201938